"It's Just Not Fair!"

- Have you ever stuck out your trembling lower lip and said, "It's just not fair"?
- Have you ever been hurt by a number-one rat fink, and then felt like you had to blab it to everyone?
- Are you angry with God for something you felt He did to you or a loved one?
- Have you ever had your very own personal pity party? For a day? For a week? For a month? For a decade?
- Are you in the midst of a crisis, feeling like you're one hair's breadth away from insanity?
- Do you struggle with deep roots of bitterness?
- Do you have a problem receiving and/or giving forgiveness?
- Have you ever felt like nobody really understands the pain you have experienced?
- Have you encountered personal tragedy some time ago and are still searching for meaning in your pain?

If you answered yes to any of these questions, *God Is Not Fair* is for you.

Before you have finished reading, you will have discovered ways to improve your course in life by making your attitude behave. You will also understand how you have already won the invisible, spiritual battle being waged this very moment for the attention of your heart.

"With wit and disarming style, Joel Freeman helps us find at least some of [the] answers."
Joni Eareckson Tada
Joni and Friends

"Freeman combines compassion and tough-minded
...ert A. Cook, 1987 President
...onal Religious Broadcasters

"God Is Not Fair"

Coming to Terms With
Life's Raw Deals

Joel A. Freeman

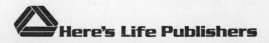

Here's Life Publishers

FIRST PRINTING, AUGUST 1987
SECOND PRINTING, MARCH 1988
THIRD PRINTING, JUNE 1988

Published by
HERE'S LIFE PUBLISHERS, INC.
P. O. Box 1576
San Bernardino, CA 92402

HLP Product No. 951905

Library of Congress Cataloging-in-Publication Data
Freeman, Joel A., 1954-
God is not fair.
1. Providence and government of God. 2. Suffering — religious aspects — Christianity. 3. Theodicy. 4. Christian life — 1960-
5. Freeman, Joel A., 1954-   . I. Title.
BT96.2.F73   1987   231'.8   87-377
ISBN 0-89840-189-5 (pbk.)

FOR MORE INFORMATION, WRITE:

L.I.F.E. — P.O. Box A399, Sydney South 2000, Australia
Campus Crusade for Christ of Canada — Box 300, Vancouver, B.C., V6C 2X3, Canada
Campus Crusade for Christ — Pearl Assurance House, 4 Temple Row, Birmingham, B2 5HG, England
Campus Crusade for Christ — P.O. Box 240, Colombo Court Post Office, Singapore 9117
Lay Institute for Evangelism — P.O. Box 8786, Auckland 3, New Zealand
Great Commission Movement of Nigeria — P.O. Box 500, Jos, Plateau State Nigeria, West Africa
Campus Crusade for Christ International — Arrowhead Springs, San Bernardino, CA 92414, U.S.A.

To my precious wife,
Laurie.

Special thanks to Ann, Delphine, Irene, Laurie, Linda, Lynn, Madeline, Melanie, and Pat, who at various times helped to translate some of my "chicken-scratchings" into legible copy. Also, thanks to those, especially Lloyd, who proofread the first drafts of the book and made helpful comments.

CONTENTS

FOREWORD

As a Christian psychiatrist, I have counseled literally hundreds of men, women, and children who have been bitterly angry at God for being unfair. The basic reason is always the same: God, in His sovereignty, either allowed or caused something to happen to these people that they would not have allowed if they were in God's position. They are angry at God for not letting them be in absolute control. This attitude stems from the basic sin of arrogance and pride.

What really astounds me is that even though I consider myself an enlightened human being who meditates on God's Word daily, I also get angry with God from time to time for not running my life circumstances the way I would like. Because I am human, I will always do this to some extent, but I have learned what to do when I develop this attitude of arrogance.

In this book, Joel Freeman does an excellent job of gently knocking the wind out of our arrogant, "God isn't fair" sails. His personal vulnerability helps us to understand that we aren't unique in having these thoughts; and he gives us an uplifting glimpse of God's overall plan, showing us that our limited understanding insufficiently qualifies us for determining what is fair or unfair.

Paul Meier, M.D.
Minirth-Meier Clinic, P.A.
Richardson, Texas

INTRODUCTION

There's a scream, "Oh my God!" Waves of panic engulf the beach. The once-quiet sunbathers point wildly. A lifeguard races toward the pounding surf. Thrashing furiously, a pair of hands suddenly reappear out of the deep. The drowning person is in an intense struggle between life and death.

Think with me for a moment. Do you identify with the drowning soul, the trained lifeguard or the powerless spectators? You are in at least one of those categories. Let me help you understand.

Right now, the state of your emotions may be saturated with sorrow and you may be grasping, like a drowning person, for answers to a multitude of "why" questions. Maybe, like the spectators, you are feeling gross inadequacies as you try to assist a friend who is hurting. Or possibly, like the lifeguard, you are in the people-helping profession. You have been through your own deep waters and are feeling used up, needing to be recharged.

- Have you ever stuck out your trembling lower lip and said, "It's just not fair"?
- Have you ever been hurt by a number-one rat fink, and then felt like you had to blab it to everyone?
- Are you angry with God for something you felt He did to you or a loved one?
- Have you ever had your very own personal pity party? For a day? For a week? For a month? For a decade?
- Are you in the midst of a crisis, feeling like you're one hair's breadth away from insanity?
- Do you struggle with deep roots of bitterness?
- Do you have a problem receiving and/or giving forgiveness?
- Have you ever felt like nobody really understands the pain you have experienced?
- Have you encountered personal tragedy some time ago and are still searching for meaning in your pain?

If you answered yes to any of these questions, this book is for you. God understands your tolerance level for suffering, and He wants to make you a tough person with a tender heart.

"Oh, no, not another negative, hell-fire-and-brimstone book!" I hear someone groan. You're absolutely right: This isn't one of those.

"But what about the title? I always thought God was fair." Hold on just a moment . . .

11

"Fair" is a fine word, but as you will see, the genuine meaning has been distorted. To help clarify its meaning, the word "fair" is set off by quotation marks throughout the book.

Before you have finished reading, you will have discovered ways to improve your course in life by making your attitude behave. You will also understand how you have already won the invisible, spiritual battle being waged this very moment for the attention of your heart.

Let's go . . .

Joel A. Freeman, M.S.
P.O. Box 2757
Columbia, Maryland 21045

"I Never Want to Hurt This Bad Again"

*All horrors have followed the same course, getting
worse and forcing you into a kind of bottleneck till,
at the very moment when you thought you must
be crushed, behold! You were out of the narrows
and all was suddenly well. The extraction hurt
more and more and then the tooth was out. The
dream became a nightmare and then you awoke.
You die and die and then you are beyond death.*

C.S. Lewis

Why are there fleas? Have you ever asked that question? No? (Obviously you've never owned a cat or dog.) Well, just think about it. What purpose do they serve? Granted, their existence creates the jobs necessary in the conception, testing, manufacturing and marketing of anti-flea shampoos and sprays. But why are they here on this planet? They are dirty and nasty and they reproduce at an incredible rate. Why did God deliberately create such seemingly unnecessary pests? Why do they exist? Is there an answer?

In the same breath we could ask: Why is there pain? You know, gut-wrenching grief and sorrow? Does it have any meaning? Let's face it, life presents many challenges to all of us.

Some people piously portray emotional pain as a brilliant blessing in disguise that really is our best friend. Somehow pain is supposed to be a useful tool, teaching us valuable lessons.

That philosophy seems rather hollow and empty, however, when talking with people who are in the throes of pain or

13

who have endured hardship. What about a couple who loses their long-awaited newborn child three days after birth, or the man who has discovered the ugly realities about his lingering, crippling disease, or the woman who has experienced an inexplicable series of tragedies? What should we say when they ask, "Why is this happening to me?" Or how do we respond when they plead, "Please help me — I never want to hurt this bad again."

I think of a woman named Germaine. She is modestly attractive. A woman in her late forties with tired, worn lines on her face. The circles around her eyes are puffy and red from recent tears.

You can perceive her discomfort and occasional embarrassment with the subject matter as she haltingly describes her life in an unrehearsed manner. Listening intently, you realize that her husband, Phil, to whom she has been married for twenty-seven years, recently left her. It hadn't been easy, but together they raised three children and pushed them through college.

They had struggled together to attain the dreams they had shared regarding their family, church and business. Now it was all gone. All her dreams were smashed when she discovered that her husband had happily moved in with a cute, young woman on the other side of town. As if her husband's departure weren't enough to deal with, Germaine is angered by the scandalous remarks being made by neighbors and acquaintances.

Certain songs on the radio, certain restaurants, and certain memories all form a conspiracy, haunting her with the fact that she was once with her husband. But now she is a separated woman facing a dark, complicated future all alone. The quiet, gnawing pain is there — always present. She looks at you inquisitively, not with a clenched fist but with a searching heart. "Why did Phil leave me? Is there something wrong with me? What should I do?"

You pause. What do you say? You try to form words out of hastily collected thoughts. Without another moment escaping she adds, "I sometimes feel so confused and helpless. And I used to handle tough situations so well." Her emotional level rises slightly, "I can't compete with his girlfriend. It's really not 'fair'! I feel like such a fool. I gave Phil the best years of my life." She pauses and reflects, while looking away, "All I know right now is that the pain is so bad at times that I can hardly stand it."

What do you tell her? Should you try to reassure her that everything will work out? That the good guys always win? That justice will prevail in the end?

In a similar vein, what would you say to Frank? He and his wife have struggled with the guilt and frustration resulting from raising a son in what they thought was a caring, well-structured home environment, only to have a police officer inform them that their son was in jail. The charges? Possession of narcotics, breaking and entering, possession of stolen goods, and resisting arrest.

Frank is understandably confused. He knew in advance that there were no iron-clad guarantees that came with child-rearing, but this took him by complete surprise. You listen carefully as he says, "Where did we go wrong as parents? We didn't pamper him. We read most of the books by Dr. Dobson and others on the subject. I tried to be a good father. You know, I took off extra time from work to go camping and fishing with him. We tried to instill proper moral and spiritual values in him. I can't understand why he would do this. I feel like a total failure." He winces as tears fill his eyes and he starts to sob, "I can't begin to tell you how much it hurts!"

A child is conceived in ecstasy, but birthed with much pain. The sharpest, hottest tears of a parent, however, are not caused by physical pain. They are the result of a sorrow that is more deeply rooted in the human soul than the body — the pain of a broken heart. And that is the way it is with life. Ideas and dreams are conceived with great enthusiasm, but the implementation of those concepts invites suffering and pain.

Some people are bombarded with heartache and tragedy, while others appear to navigate through life hardly touched by difficulty. Yet everyone endures emotional pain. Suffering is a universal language.

I know that language. Like Germaine and Frank, I have felt my own emotional pain while crying out, "I never want to hurt this bad again."

Over the years, I have become more understanding of and patient with people who rail out against God in the midst of personal trauma. You see, I too have asked similar questions and made similar statements when placed in the crucible of "unfair" circumstances. When in those situations, I have been shocked by the depths of rage I have been capable of experiencing.

In future chapters I will relate some of my own struggles and will share time-tested principles that have sustained me before, during and after "unfair" events that have left my emotional system raw and bleeding and in a state of shock.

But first, you are about to meet an unusual group of people in a rather unique drama.

DISCUSSION GUIDE

1. Have you ever gone through a painful, hurtful experience that caused you to question the "fairness" of God? Think back on the specifics of the situation and try to remember what your inner-most feelings were at that time.

2. Your past, present and future "unfair" experiences are prime candidates for God's healing. As you read "God Is Not Fair," ask Him to help you apply the principles you will be learning.

CHAPTER 2

Cosmic Killjoy

I still rebel and complain against God; I cannot keep from groaning. How I wish I knew where to find him, and knew how to go where he is. I would state my case before him and present all the arguments in my favor. I want to know what he would say and how he would answer me.

(Job 23:1-5, GNB)

Picture this: A convocation of grumpy people meeting on a hillside to have a gripe session with God.

The first person to make his case is Moses. He firmly grasps his cane and takes an authoritative step forward. He looks dramatically to his left. His gaze then sweeps to the right. He pauses deliberately, stroking his flowing beard. He looks directly at God, and booms in a Charlton Heston-type voice, "God, we've known each other quite well. You did a great job with the Red Sea and Pharaoh's army. Really now, couldn't I have at least taken one step into the land of Canaan? I have been nursing a grudge against You for a few thousand years. I must get something off my chest. My experience with You hasn't been totally pleasant. You deliberately built me up, just to let me down. All I did was hit the rock! What's the big deal?

"Hey listen," Moses continues with his voice rising in emotion, "I gave up the comforts of Egypt as Pharaoh's number-

17

two man. I followed You without question. All I got in return was forty years on the backside of a lousy desert, forty additional years of dealing with a multitude of people who behaved like thankless morons, and then I died just thirty days before everybody else went into the Promised Land! I'm disgusted with You. You're simply not 'fair'!"

God smiles reverently and silently nods to the next in line.

John the Baptist clears his throat, nervously looking at a crumpled piece of paper clutched in his hand. He begins, "God, I know You are righteous and holy, *but* I am really annoyed with You. The more I think about it, the madder I get. Let me ask You a question: Have You ever had to eat grasshoppers? I had to — YUK! Furthermore, You commanded me to trudge over hill and dale, yelling about repentance at the top of my lungs. And that's not all! After working so hard for You, I ended up in a prison cell and then unceremoniously got my head lopped off! It just isn't 'fair'! I believe You exploited me for Your personal gain. Is that the way You operate? Do You enjoy squeezing people for all You can get out of them and then delight in spitting them out? Huh? Is that what You do?"

God smiles disarmingly and nods to another individual. This one carries himself with an aristocrat's bearing. His name is Job. He brushes his nose with his finger and speaks. "God, I know You have almost everything under control. *But,* I believe You are a 'cosmic killjoy.' You must sit on Your throne, waiting until someone is enjoying life to the fullest. Then, You must break into sinister laughter and wring Your hands gleefully. I can see it clearly; then what You do is smash everything that person owns. Don't try to back out of this one; I'm here personally to attest to the fact that this is a favorite pastime of Yours."

At this point, everyone nods vigorously and grunts affirmatively.

Job continues, "I was a helpless victim. Without consulting me, You gave the devil permission to rip me apart. I lost 7,000 sheep, 3,000 camels, my oxen, donkeys, servants, seven sons, and my three precious daughters. That's not all; while I was sitting in the ashes of my burned-out house, nursing my boils, my wife told me that I had lost my integrity, and that I should curse You and die. God, I don't even begin to understand why this happened to me. You are 'unfair' in Your dealings, not only with me, but with every person who walks on the face of the earth!"

As God looks down the line, He sees many people whose tempers are rising. John is complaining about his "Social Security benefits" on the insane-asylum island called Patmos. The other disciples are griping about their disconcerting experiences with martyrdom. Jeremiah complains about the dungeon conditions, where he had mud practically up to his ears.

Paul has a long list to grumble about: He was shipwrecked three times, naked, hungry, bitterly persecuted, stoned, rejected by the religious system, jailed, and finally killed. Joseph is steaming mad because he was sold as a slave, framed by the boss's wife, and thrown in jail. His only crime was a dream! Honest, pure Stephen still has lumps and bruises from being stoned to death.

Also, God can't overlook David. He was hunted like an animal by jealous Saul. Then, after thirty minutes of sin with Bathsheba, David reaped literal havoc within his family and kingdom for forty years. Each one has a briefcase full of "facts" that justify his primary complaint: *God is not "fair."*

As I depict the preceding scene, I do so with my tongue firmly planted in my cheek. But I am completely serious about this one point: Every human, at one time or another, asks the following sixty-million-dollar questions — "If God is a God of love, why is there so much suffering in the world? Why do the wicked seem to prosper? Why do terrible things happen to nice people? Why does life have to hurt so much? Isn't there an easier way to grow? Can any meaning be found in suffering?"

There are no glib answers to these universal questions. In fact, volumes have been written in an effort to address each question specifically. Many of these books assist in providing a measure of comfort to those in the midst of gut-wrenching trials.

I will not attempt to provide generic-brand solutions to problems that have vexed thinkers for centuries. In his booklet, *Why Does God Allow Suffering?*, Paul Malte explains:

> The Bible itself never offers very easy answers to suffering, or to sufferers. Even in Job, the classic book on suffering, the problem of evil is never explained away. But, Job does learn to live with suffering — and with the Lord Creator. Deep in his soul — not his mind — Job discovers the peace which transcends all human under-

standing. Jesus — who claims to be God's representative
among men — never unties the intellectual problem of
God's goodness and God's power. He simply acts to
demonstrate the Father's goodness and His power chan-
neled personally to people. Jesus does not heal all the
lepers in Palestine, exorcise all unclean spirits, make
whole all marriages. Wherever and whenever He can, He
heals and He helps. He gives people the inner attitude,
the courage and joy, to handle suffering. He does nothing
to ward off His own death, and He becomes the victim
of human hostility. He suffers both the anguish of physical
death and the hell of alienation from God. By suffering
with us He suffers for us. He suffers so that our suffering
might be transformed and transcended into triumph.

Christians have no tidy answers to suffering, no easy
ten principles for happy sufferers. They only have attitudes
for meeting it, handles for overcoming it, outlooks for
transcending it.[1]

A major blockage to enjoying life to the fullest is the
"fairness" question. Every home has been invaded by the
"fairness" issue. You know the scene — little Mary comes running into the house at curfew, and says, "How come Johnny
gets to stay outside for another hour? Why do I have to go
to bed? Mom, you're not 'fair'!"

Our children can't see the bigger picture. When they get
married and have children of their own, they soon understand
some of the reasons for their parents' "because-I-told-you-so"
decisions. They eventually realize that love motivates parents
to make choices that aren't always consistent with the wishes
and timing of children.

No two children are created with equal talents, mental
capacities, or physical opportunities. Sibling rivalry can develop
when a younger child follows an athletic big brother or popular
big sister in school. It is not "fair" when they are constantly
referred to as "Jim's younger brother" or "Mary's little sister."
Friction can also result when a child of a large family consumes
sixty percent of the household income because of a periodic
illness. It's not "fair" when the sickness of one child governs
the lifestyle of the entire family.

Every soccer field and Little League diamond has hosted
angry parents who are disgruntled with their children's lack
of playing time. These parents exhibit unhealthy role models
in front of their children. The theme of "fairness" characterizes

their attitudes as they second-guess the coach's decisions and grumble about the performance of the one who played in their child's stead.

Grades, special privileges, and difficult tasks provide many opportunities for students to harp upon the theme of "fairness" in the classroom setting. Many a harried teacher has spent agonizing moments questioning his or her ability after an intense case of verbal assault and battery from a rebellious student or reactionary parent.

Alone in his office, a businessman buries his face in his hands, frustrated over the loss of a large business deal that was won by a competitor through unethical means. He doesn't mind losing an account, but not as a result of unscrupulous business practices. It's not "fair."

Every pastor who is worth his salt has struggled with God's apparent lack of "fairness." Undue criticism and pressure are a part of the real estate when one enters into a position of leadership. The pastor who knows what it's like to draw up into a fetal position on the office floor and sob until there are no tears left is a man who can be mightily used by God if he dares to settle the "fairness" question.

At best, a marriage will suffer from peaceful co-existence if the "fairness" issues are not squarely confronted in both lives. In recent decades, the divorce rate has skyrocketed because, by and large, individuals have decided that personal pleasure and convenience take precedence over commitment. This humanistic philosophy actually mocks the bedrock values that have contributed to the stability of past generations.

The pathways to alcoholism and drug addiction are paved with the "fairness" problem. Addicted people feel that since life has dealt them a dirty deal they have the right to drown, smoke, or snort their sorrows into oblivion.

Every church has experienced the ruckus caused by some disgruntled pew-warmer. Or, what about the crabby deacon? What about the church split that was caused by a difference of opinion over the carpet color in the sanctuary? The group that vacated the premises claimed it wasn't "fair."

People who are single by choice, divorce, or death must grapple with the theme of "fairness." But they are not the only ones who fight the "fairness" question. What about the terminally ill, the handicapped, the children of divorced parents, or the abused spouses?

Is God a "cosmic killjoy," as some would have us believe?

How did the "fairness" concept start?

DISCUSSION GUIDE

1. In your opinion, is God "fair"?

2. The hypothetical gripe session with God was attended by Moses, John the Baptist, Job, Paul, Joseph, John, Jeremiah, Stephen, and David. Which biblical character do you identify with most when it comes to questioning God's "fairness"?

3. Do you recall any instances in your life when you realized that God has been more than just with you?

4. What is your yardstick of "fairness"? In relation to what?

CHAPTER 3

Sympathy
for the Devil

What we call adversity, God calls opportunity.
What we call tribulation, God calls growth.

Anonymous

Have you ever felt sorry for the devil? Maybe just a twinge of pity? After all, he was kicked out of heaven without a second chance. Isn't it true that God was abrupt and unkind in the way He handled Satan?

Without a moment's hesitation, you probably answered the preceding questions with a resounding "No!" It didn't take long for you to respond. As an intelligent being, Satan knows that most people aren't inclined to fill their crying towels with tears because of his awful plight as the fallen prince of darkness.

Most people understand that Lucifer became overly conscious of his beauty in heaven and his value to God. Many are aware that pride motivated him to make the grandiose statement found in Isaiah 14:13-14, "I will ascend to heaven and rule the angels. I will take the highest throne. I will preside on the Mount of Assembly far away in the North. I will climb to the highest heavens. I will be like the Most High."

Almost everyone has read that God, refusing to co-exist

23

with this haughty being, gave him the left foot of fellowship.
As a result, Satan was booted out of heaven like a bolt of
lightning. But he didn't leave alone; one third of all the angels
in heaven impudently acknowledged their independence of
God and followed close on Lucifer's heels.

Ever since that event in history, Satan has been boiling
mad and is driven to influence humans into thinking that God
is not "fair" in His dealings. This is all part of his massive
public relations campaign which is designed to turn creatures
against their Creator.

Satan unveiled his strategy in the Garden of Eden. In
fact, the unabridged edition of the "Freeman Translation" quotes
Lucifer as saying, "Eve, you mean to tell me that God told
you not to eat of the 'no-no' fruit? Oh, that's terrible! You must
feel so rejected. I can understand how you feel. I have had a
lot of personal experience with God. He was extremely cruel
to me. I had so much to offer, but He was only interested in
a one-man show. He really isn't 'fair.' He is threatened by
anyone who might become His equal. He probably doesn't
want you to eat the fruit because of how much you'll know
after the first bite. He wants to hold you back from advance-
ment, thereby cramping your style forever. Go ahead, take a
bite. You'll be enlightened with a new level of consciousness.
That's it — just one teensy, weensy, itsy, bitsy bite . . ."

Now that you know the scoop about what really went
on in the Garden of Eden, it is easy to comprehend the devil's
strategy in the here and now. Through precise maneuvers by
his invisible host of demons, he waits until people are in a
vulnerable state of mind, and then he hits them between the
eyes with timeless reminders like:

- God has forgotten and forsaken you.
- God doesn't love you as much as He loves other people.
- God is a hard, cruel taskmaster.
- You have committed the unpardonable sin.
- You wouldn't be hurting so badly if God had everything
under control.
- God is not "fair."

Lucifer wants to take advantage of every opportunity to
attack his former boss. He slanders and curses Him at every
turn, maliciously hoping to build his success by trying to defeat
Christ. His evil thoughts against God are blatantly exposed in
the following statements:

> I dip my forefinger in the watery blood of your impotent, mad redeemer and write over his thorn-torn brow: The true prince of evil — the king of slaves.
> I gaze into the glassy eye of your fearsome Jehovah and pluck him by the beard; I lift a broadaxe and split open his worm-eaten skull!
> Behold the crucifix: what does it symbolize? Pallid incompetence hanging on a tree . . .
> He who turns the other cheek is a cowardly dog! Self-preservation is the highest law.
> Life is the great indulgence — death, the great abstinence. Therefore, make the most of life — here and now.
> Say to thine own heart, "I am my own redeemer."[1]
>
> *The Satanic Bible*

One can clearly see that Satan is not operating under the guise of a hidden agenda. He absolutely despises Jesus Christ and will seek to destroy anyone who confesses Him as Savior and Lord.

Recently, I was reintroduced to the reality of Satan's ongoing plan to sabotage God's character by promoting the "fairness" concept to humans. While driving across town to visit friends one rainy evening, the soaked form of a hitchhiker suddenly appeared in the beam of my headlight.

Being a former hitchhiker, I instinctively screeched to a halt. A young man in his early twenties climbed in, thanking me profusely. His smile was framed by rather long, damp hair. We proceeded on our way, introducing ourselves and exchanging a few pleasantries. Taking advantage of the opportunity to share Christ with him, I waited for a few moments and then nonchalantly inquired, "Fred, are you interested in spiritual things?"

I was not prepared for his answer. In an even tone, he informed me, "Yeah, I am. I've been studying the occult for several years now." Intrigued, I feigned naiveté by asking him questions that gently probed the depth of his involvement. At first he answered in a guarded manner, but then he began to share more freely. I soon discovered the seriousness of his dedication to the devil's cause.

As we drove on, I asked Fred to explain the circumstances that led up to and followed Lucifer's grand exit from heaven. Without hesitation, he graphically described God's injustice in dealing with Satan. He went on to explain that Satan had a legitimate gripe against a God who was jealous, cruel, and "unfair" in the way He had handled the devil.

As we conversed, two predominant thoughts entered my mind. I remembered an event that occurred on a Thursday evening in 1974, an event so significant that it is indelibly etched in my memory. As a group of fervent Bible college students, we were gathered for an evening of theological discussion and prayer. About fifty people were present. Suddenly the evening was shattered by the actions and utterances of a woman who had come to visit the school for a week.

I am very cautious about attributing abnormal human behavior to satanic activity, but this woman's words and actions were indicative of demonic possession. At the precise moment when we confronted her with the name and power of Jesus, she reacted violently — kicking, cursing, and biting. At times she had to be restrained by two muscular men.*

"You all think you're so smart," she screamed in an unearthly voice, "Well, I want you to know that we are more powerful. We are winning. We have control over the whole world."

A cold, involuntary shiver pulsated up and down my spine as the reality of kingdom warfare hit me full in the face.

Her darkened eyes narrowed as she dramatically surveyed everyone in the room. For a brief, eternal moment our eyes met and then disengaged. She proudly tossed her head, clearing the black, bushy hair from the sides of her sweaty face and seethed, "I hate every one of you. I hate you all."

As the night wore on, she spoke in several different voices on everything from drugs to the subject of "666," the mark of the beast. Sometimes her words came in guttural tones, others in soft and mellow voices, while others were punctuated with a combination of high-pitched shrieks.

One statement, however, penetrated my memory on this rainy evening in the car with the hitchhiker. One of her utterances had come in a pitifully haunting voice: "It is not 'fair.' You get many chances, but we got only one chance."

---

* (Author's note: In my opinion, this incident was an actual case of demon possession. The majority of cases, however, that involve individuals having bizarre psychotic breaks with reality, may actually be people suffering from a dopamine imbalance in the brain. They may hear voices or even experience visual hallucinations. Many times this is correctable by proper doses of Thorazine. A Christian psychiatrist should be consulted.)

As I drove through the rain I also remembered the title of a rock song popularized by a musical group called The Rolling Stones. The reality of the title of the song, "Sympathy for the Devil," had a chilling effect on me. As we continued our ride, I was able to recall some of its lyrics:

Please allow me to introduce myself:
I'm a man of wealth of taste.
I've been around for long, long years —
Stolen many a man's soul and faith.
I was around when Jesus Christ
Had his moment of doubt and faith.
I made damn sure that Pilate
Washed his hands, and sealed his fate.

Pleased to meet you,
Hoped you guessed my name.
But what's puzzling you
Is the nature of my game . . .

. . . Just as every cop is a criminal
And all the sinners, Saints
As heads is tails, just call me Lucifer
'Cause I'm in need of some restraint.
So, if you meet me have some courtesy;
Have some sympathy and some taste.
Use all your well-learned politesse
Or I'll lay your soul to waste![2]

As I reflected on these thoughts, Satan's strategy became much clearer. With each passing moment, Fred was verifying my suspicions as he tried to impress me as to why Satan had received the raw end of the deal. We were just warming up to the subject at hand when he suddenly interjected, "I've got to get off at this next exit."

In the darkness, I fumbled around in the pouch under the driver's seat and hastily pulled out a gospel tract, handing it to him. "Fred, I'm interested in your thoughts about God and Satan," I said. "Your comments tonight show that you have been thinking deeply about spiritual things. Please accept this piece of paper from me. It will explain God's power to forgive your sins and give you a brand-new perspective about life."

I pulled the car over just after the exit ramp and asked him to have an "Elijah Showdown." "What's that?" he quizzed, laughing slightly, with his hand on the door handle.

"Well, Fred," I continued, "There's a story in the Bible about the prophet Elijah who bragged that his God was true and that the god, Baal, was false. Elijah then proposed that two altars be built on top of a mountain and that the real god would pour fire down from the sky. The prophets of Baal took him up on the challenge with thousands of people gathered around, waiting for the fireworks."

Knowing that I had a limited amount of time, I paused momentarily to see if he was still interested or if I was boring him to tears. Sensing what I was doing, Fred took his hand off the door handle and responded, "Go on. Then what happened?"

"Well, the prophets of Baal danced around for hours and nothing happened." With his expressed interest, I slowed down a bit. "When Elijah prayed, fire instantly came down and God showed that He was the only true God. Fred," I said softly, "God wants to prove to you that He is still the only true God. Satan is real and he has a lot of power as you well know. But he has fed you a bunch of lies about what happened way back when he was kicked out of heaven. God is more powerful. Don't just take my word for it. Prove it for yourself by asking Jesus to come into your life and be your personal Savior. His blood was poured out on the cross so that people like you and me can receive the free gift of eternal life. I'd like to see you come on the winning side."

There was an odd silence. And then he commented, "Thanks, Joel, you've given me a lot to think about." He paused again for a few seconds, opened the door and then turned to me, saying, "Thanks for the ride."

I sped off into the rainy night, hoping that somehow our conversation had made an impact on Fred's life. I know it did on mine.

Just like Fred, King David's friend, Asaph, swallowed the "fairness" concept — hook, line, and sinker. Asaph began to think that God was unjust in His dealings with people. In Psalm 73, Asaph compared his life with that of the wicked. According to his evaluation, the unrighteous enjoyed their lives to the fullest. They conducted unprincipled business practices and unabashedly flaunted their evil lifestyles, yet they had no glaring problems. They were so fat and prosperous that their eyes almost popped out of their sockets.

Asaph was almost sucked into Satan's "bad attitude" strategy against God until he went into the sanctuary. It was there that he saw objective truth as it really was. He had become contaminated by worldly thinking and had compared his situation with the lifestyles of others. Up to this point, he didn't see the bigger picture of eternal value. But in the sanctuary, his mind became clear, and he could say, "'There's none on earth I desire besides Thee, O LORD" (Psalm 73:25).

Knowing full well that the "fairness" theme was prevalent, the apostle Paul was careful to address the issue when talking about Jacob and Esau in Romans 9. Many scholars speculate regarding the reasons why God loved Jacob but hated Esau. Paul simply asked, "Is there unrighteousness (injustice) with God?" His take-it-or-leave-it answer was, "God forbid" — or in modern day English, "Heavens to Betsy, no!"

I am not a foaming-at-the-mouth, witch-hunting, there's-a-devil-in-your-closet demon chaser. But I am absolutely convinced of the fact that Satan has an organized host of commanding and commissioned officers. These foul spirits are united by the distorted belief that they can destroy the kingdom of God.

It may sound weird, but Satan's desire is to get human beings to feel sorry for him as the underdog in his campaign against God. Granted, it's a tough assignment for the Public Relations Department in hell. But the way he is trying to accomplish this mammoth task is by amplifying God's apparent lack of "fairness" when earth-shaking events occur on a personal basis or on a worldwide scale.

The automatic result is that our childlike trust in God's character as the sovereign ruler of the universe is at best eroded, or at worst, smashed. We become disillusioned with God and then we enter into a phase whereby we frantically search for happiness without consulting God's guidance. Of course, our search for happiness does not produce the desired results, so our disillusionment with God and the people who follow Him intensifies.

Over a period of time, Satan capitalizes on our natural bent toward rationalization and bitterness, and we end up with a mere plastic shell of religion that lacks substance and power. Slowly but surely, our understanding becomes darkened, and we fall prey to man-centered ideals that leave God totally out of the picture. We are now available to accept any form of deception as truth because something is missing.

DISCUSSION GUIDE

1. As you look back on your life, think of two situations in the past two years where Satan tried to convince you that God was "unfair" during those times. Have developments since then caused you to modify your attitudes at all?

2. In retrospect, can you identify at least one positive attribute in your life that God has developed through those unpleasant experiences?

3. According to Romans 5:1-5, why do you think God allows hardship into a person's life?

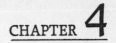

Adjust
to the Justice
of God

*God does not mock His children with a night
that has no ending; and to every man who stands
resolute while the darkness lasts, there comes at
length the vindication of faith and the breaking of
the day.*

James S. Stewart

At this moment I can hear someone in the middle of a swamp, up to his tail in alligators, yelling, "Hey, wait a minute! How does the 'fairness' issue affect me, and how can I avoid being a sucker for the devil's tactics?" I'm so glad he asked.

Most people are bona fide, card-carrying members of the Navel Gazing Society (N.G.S.). You haven't heard of it? I'm surprised. Pause momentarily and think about the last time you made an utter fool of yourself. Maybe you inadvertently opened your mouth and blabbed some stupid comment in the presence of important guests.

Did you feel a sudden rush of embarrassment? Later that evening, did you toss to and fro in bed as the little theater in your brain played the disgusting scene over and over again? Did you cry yourself to sleep? Was the following week wrecked because of periodic preoccupation with that particular upsetting event?

The more you analyzed, the deeper you went into depression. You may have been able to explain the psychological ramifications brilliantly, but you couldn't seem to step out of the vicious cycle. As a longstanding, distinguished member of N.G.S., I can understand. You see, I too, have suffered from the paralysis of self-analysis.

As I sit here at my writing desk reminiscing over some awkward, uncomfortable moments, I feel the flush of slight embarrassment. What about the time I preached a whole sermon and, well, I'd rather not say where, but a zipper that was supposed to be closed was — um — open? And the message was so good! What about the time I told a bald-headed joke to a bald-headed man? He tried to strangle me — well, almost. Or the time I went to the hospital, visiting a young boy who had just undergone an operation on his appendix and when I left, without thinking, I affectionately patted his stomach while saying good-bye, causing him to double over with a painful howl? His mother's smile of gratitude for my visit turned into a look of horror and panic.

Each time, I suffered for weeks as an official member of N.G.S., being overwhelmed periodically with depression and extreme self-consciousness at the mere thought of the disconcerting events. It wasn't till much later that the seriousness of the situations abated and a glimmer of humor slipped in with a degree of objectivity.

Something that has never ceased to amaze me, though, is how sudden situations give rise to instant feelings of anger, inferiority, retaliation, and self-justification. These feelings may have been masked in a pressure-free, predictable environment, but given the unexpected, we impulsively are at the mercy of the spasmodic reactions of our emotions.

First the bad news. Our hearts are deceitful and desperately wicked. God knows it, the Bible says it, and we profess it. But we are greatly surprised when the condition of our hearts gets exposed in unexpected situations. These are sovereignly designed circumstances that don't afford us the luxury of a pre-planned response. We react foolishly and then spend hours beating ourselves up, wondering why we allowed ourselves to go out of control. The answer is simple. Careful self-analysis may offer a more detailed explanation, but when all the smoke finally clears, we see that disguised selfishness and pride were the causes of our reaction.

The greater the trial, the more intense the pain. The

greater the pain, the more we tend to question God's purpose. God, however, doesn't fall off His throne in utter shock when we yell at Him. He can handle abusive language and any number of fists shaken menacingly in His direction. He understands, and patiently waits until we have exhausted our show of bravado. He is not threatened. His caring attitude does not change. He realizes that the heavenly complaint department will always be full of angry callers screaming, *"God is not fair!"*

I was on that line years ago, yelling at God between sobs. My nineteen-year-old heart had been broken by devastating news. The message was clear. In no uncertain terms, my girlfriend had said, "Joel, you're going to make a fine husband for some woman, but I'm not that woman." She had communicated it nicely and firmly. But all I could hear between her careful words was, "Beat it. Scram. Get out of my life, you no-good piece of junk. Consider yourself rejected. You are worthless. Do yourself a favor — go play in the traffic!"

In that moment of truth, I was frantic, searching madly for some reason and logic in it all. Nothing could console me. My best friend, Scot, couldn't help. Everything was hopeless. I felt like a helpless little puppy, numb after a severe beating.

As humans, we are fragile creatures — always one hair's breadth away from insanity. Yet at the same time it is a paradox, because we are a stubborn, rebellious lot. Each new level of growth seems to be accompanied by much weeping and gnashing of teeth. We artfully plant our heels in the dirt, trying desperately to maintain the comfort zones we have so diligently established. At such times God brings in the demolition experts. He permits certain trials that gently blast us into the next spiritual ZIP code. We despise these afflictions and view them as nasty, uncalled-for pests (like fleas), but much later we say, "You know what? I now think I can understand why that had to happen. It was necessary and above all it was good for me. I'm much better because of it."

"Hey, where's the good news?" I can hear our swampy piece of alligator bait ask. Hold on just a minute. Before continuing, we must understand a fundamental principle: *God is in control.* Absolutely nothing can happen to us or to anyone else without His consent. Even the devil has to check with God before he can cause disease, separation, or destruction. (As he did in the case of Job, for example.) Satan doesn't like the rules of this game. In his opinion, the rules are not "fair" because they are not in his favor.

Do you think Satan and his demons are depressed about what Christ did on Calvary? Of course they are! After all, Jesus defeated the works of the devil. Through His blood, we are now accepted by the Father. Misery loves company. If we buy into it, Satan will cause us to feel exactly what he feels, think what he thinks, and say what he says about God's lack of "fairness."

"Fairness" reduces God's standards to the place where we can perform and function in life without utter, total dependence on Him. Complicating matters, "fairness" demands that we take time to clarify and evaluate circumstances from the limited perspective of each person involved, rather than from God's eternal viewpoint. As a direct product of humanistic philosophy, the "fairness" doctrine is based on man's value system and timetable. "Fairness" causes us to gaze at our navels and evaluate others from a subjective perspective. "Fairness" is incubated in hell.

The elder son's attitude illustrates the "fairness" focus in the story that Jesus told, commonly known as the Parable of the Prodigal Son (Luke 15:11-32). As the son walked in from another hard day of work in the field, he heard some festive music and observed some energetic dancing. Upon closer inspection, he discovered that all this merriment was in honor of his wayward younger brother's return from a distant country, where he had lived a life filled with wine, women, and song.

In so many words, he said, "Hey, this isn't 'fair'! All these years I've lived in the straight and narrow way. I've always been punctual and I've always been an honest worker, with a good, clean life. Yet, a party has never been thrown for me! My kid brother acts like a fool, runs away from home and spends his entire inheritance. And when he returns home, dad empties the bank account to give him the royal treatment. What's a guy gotta do to get some attention around here? Backslide? Be honest with me. Does this look 'fair' to you?"

Since God isn't "fair" as humans perceive "fairness," what is the alternative? Could we please have a drum roll? Now for the good news: God is actually merciful and just. Satan does not want us to understand and apply this truth in everyday life. God is eternally motivated by justice. Regardless of how rampant sin is on the earth, God's justice prevails. The principles of justice are universal, being the same in the center of a busy marketplace in Shanghai, as they are in the darkest corner of New York City. His justice is not optional and knows no time boundaries. And since God has the first and last word as the King of kings and Lord of lords, human beings who choose not to follow the precepts of His justice, fall into deep trouble. Some may seem to escape the consequences while on earth, but will stand naked before Him at the Judgment Seat of Christ. There, all the hidden things of the heart will be pulled out from the shadows of human reasons and excuses. His truth prevails. Nothing escapes the ultimate justice of God.

God perfectly knows everything. He knows the focused direction of the hearts of every person who has ever lived on this ancient spaceship called earth. He sees everything. He shows no favoritism. Justice reveals God's true nature of love and, at the same time, reveals the rebellious nature of man, which is placed on exhibit. Therefore, justice establishes guilt when God's standards in His Word are violated.

Recently, I encountered an example of the nature of God's justice while studying a few verses in the book of Revelation. I had always believed that God poured out His wrath upon habitually wicked people only after His temper rose to the boiling point. It was then, I had believed, that God unleashed His rage upon arrogant sinners when He could tolerate the pressure no longer. Boy, was I in for a surprise! Let's refer to a few of the verses that exhibit the wrath of God during the tribulation period.

> And the kings of the earth . . . said to the mountains and rocks, "Fall on us, and hide us from the face of Him that sitteth on the throne, and from the wrath [orgē] of the Lamb: For the great day of His wrath [orgē] is come; and who shall be able to stand?"
> Revelation 6:15-17

I better understood God's justice upon the discovery of two main words in the original Greek language that are translated "wrath" in the book of Revelation. The word *thumos*[1] indicates a turbulent outburst of hot wrath which erupts from an inward indignation. This word emphasizes a boiling agitation or commotion that is subject to sudden rises in emotion. It can be used to describe an individual who is usually considerate, but when given a certain set of upsetting circumstances can lose his or her temper in an explosive manner.

The other term of significance that is translated "wrath" in Revelation is *orgē*[2] which denotes wrath in the sense of anger and vengeance. This suggests more of an abiding, settled attitude. In summary, *thumos* is the boiling agitation of the emotions while *orgé* is a settled habit of mind.

In the book of Revelation, *orge* is always indicated when God's wrath is mentioned. This reveals an important aspect about the implementation of His justice in the way He deals with His created beings. He has always retained and will always retain a settled hatred against sin, coupled with a permanent love for righteousness.

In other words, God does not "lose His temper." Nor does He take vengeance in an unjust, knee-jerk manner. God's hatred of wickedness has always been eternally present in His nature. During the Tribulation period He still maintains the same settled attitude regarding sin and righteousness that He has retained throughout each event in human history, including the way in which He dealt with Lucifer before his fall from heaven. He functions objectively, which enables Him to cause the sun to rise on the evil and the good each day and to send the much-needed rain for the crops of the righteous and unrighteous (Matthew 5:45).

No appeals mixed with "fairness" logic will change His mindset. His justice stands, regardless of the situational ethics or extenuating circumstances. "Fairness" tries to remove guilt, usually by mocking principles set forth in God's Word or by shifting the blame. ("I act the way I do because my mother forced me to eat porridge when I was a kid.") Justice, however, states that we are individually responsible for our internal attitudes and external behavior. Taking responsibility is the first giant step toward mental, emotional and spiritual health.

This is where mercy comes riding in as our knight in shining armor. Through the eyes of mercy, He looks beyond our faults and sees our needs, patiently viewing us as finished products — even while we are in process. Mercy is given to those who agree with God's standards of righteousness, but then immediately confess their inability to achieve those standards. This, however, requires adjustments on our part.

As an avid downhill skier, I have been following the latest technology in ski bindings. On an average run, skis undergo a tremendous amount of flex. Obviously, this causes the bindings to alternately separate slightly and then press hard against the soles of the boots, depending upon the position of the skis. Within recent years, bindings have been designed to adjust with the skis so that the same pressure is always applied against the boots, thereby ensuring greater safety for the bones of the skier.

This exemplifies a truth about us. Romans 12:2 claims that we are continually transformed when our minds spiritually adjust to God's way of thinking in the midst of extreme pressure such as when a home burns down or when disillusionment strikes because of an unfulfilled desire or when personal failure invites one into the paralysis of analysis or when a prisoner is denied parole or when a loved one finds that he or she is in the advanced stages of an incurable disease or when a bright young man is accidentally hit by a car and is paralyzed from the neck down or when a top executive has a heart attack or when a teen-aged son or daughter is arrogantly rebellious or when a wife discovers her husband has been unfaithful or when one's finances are out of control or when a woman has been raped.

In these moments of severe flex we have options:

1. to go crazy;
2. to commit suicide;
3. to adjust to God's way of thinking.

These are all real-life situations that smash us to the ground as crumpled forms of humanity. At first we are shocked. We deny it has happened to us. We weep until we experience "dry heaves." Motivated by anger, we then strike out at the ones we love the most, frantically searching for meaning in our pain. When all natural strength is abated, somehow we are ushered into the awesome presence of God. There is a gentle, sweet communication with Him. Struggle ceases; we accept.

What has happened is that we have adjusted to the justice of God. We have entered into a new phase of fellowship with Him. Does it always have to happen this dramatically? No, but many times it does. It depends how deeply God has chosen to cut into the core of our hearts.

But how do we adjust to His justice? In a later chapter, we will discover how Job settled the "fairness" question and adjusted to God's mercy and justice, but I'll give you a sneak preview. After Job was confronted with the great power of God, he realized how small he and his problems were. He immediately was made painfully aware of his dire need for God's mercy. His former questions about God's "fairness" were not specifically answered by God. Rather, Job was overwhelmed by the revelation of God's presence. Automatically, questions were no longer a big deal for Job and he adjusted to God's justice. Nothing changed except Job's mind. In the end he had no problems extending mercy to his three judgmental buddies, and God gave him a double blessing.

In the midst of pain, our emotions run wild. That is why we desperately need a crash diet of objective assistance from the Scriptures. Here in the 20th century, we adjust to the justice of God by having a categorical understanding about God. It is also important for us to understand His intentions for us because when we are hurting, we generally put His motives on trial and question His integrity.

Some may say, "But God is so mysterious, no one can really know who He is!" While it is true that God is so great that no human thought can fully contain Him, we do have the ability to know God. Our responsibility is to pump the knowledge we do have about God into our minds and then ask the Holy Spirit to make it a living reality in good times as well as bad.

The following attributes of God are primed and ready to be pumped into your think tank right now. Ready?

1. *God knows everything (Acts 15:18).*
2. *God is holy* (1 Peter 1:15,16). He gives you the power to walk in the light.
3. *God is love* (1 John 4:8). He is vitally interested in your welfare.
4. *God is true* (Romans 3:4). He keeps all agreements without grumbling behind your back.
5. *God answers to no one* (Isaiah 40:13-14). What God does for you is not out of a sense of obligation.
6. *God is all powerful* (Revelation 19:6). You can be secure in His care for you.
7. *God is infinite and eternal* (Psalms 90:2). He has the perfect viewpoint concerning your suffering.
8. *God is unchanging and unchangeable* (James 1:17). He is not schizophrenic in His compassionate attitude toward you.
9. *God is everywhere present* (Psalms 139:1-24). You cannot escape His work in your life.

10. *God is righteous and just* (Psalms 19:9).
He is no respector of persons.
11. *God is the number-one Ruler in the universe* (Ephesians 1:1-23). He has everything
under control, including your situation.

Many times we want God to adjust to our way of
thinking. When this is our approach, it doesn't take long for
us to realize that we are engaged in an exercise of futility. If,
however, we adjust properly to God's thoughts, we will increase
in value to Him as His servants here on earth. We can then
step outside our wounds and bring the healing power of the
cross of Jesus Christ to others who are hurting. We have
categorically adjusted to God's way of thinking.

Bluntly put, God will not adjust to your way of thinking.
You may try to manipulate His attention through weeping,
pleading, or backsliding. But after all is said and done, you
will adjust to His thoughts revealed in the Word.

You may blow off steam and act like a fool for a while,
but sooner or later, after total exhaustion, you must reckon
with the fact that He will not budge. He is in charge. He is
the Creator. You are His creature. Humble Christians have no
argument with this reality, because once they understand it,
they enter into great freedom, living and loving within the
boundary lines of their spiritual inheritance.

DISCUSSION GUIDE

1. What is the basic difference between "fairness" and
justice?

2. In what ways could you adjust to God's sovereignty
if your spouse or best friend died suddenly in an automobile
accident?

3. How teachable are you?

CHAPTER 5

Don't
Lose Your Spit
and Vinegar

*Adversity does not make us frail; it only shows
us how frail we are.*

Abraham Lincoln

*S*pit and vinegar: the resolve to win and succeed in
spite of all odds; clenched teeth, gritted in dogged determination; eyes blazing with purpose, eternal purpose; the refusal
to compromise godly convictions; despising the easier road,
the path of least resistance; that substance which makes one
unwilling to retire from the sometimes painful process of
growth even if everything seems to be totally "unfair"; the
disdain for self-pity and prolonged periods of personal discouragement.

What does it take for you to lose your will to fight?
What "unfair" event or series of "unfair" circumstances can
force you to consider quitting and throwing in the towel?

It happened to Jeremiah. He lost his spit and vinegar.
He was a weeping prophet, aware of the backslidden condition
of the nation of Israel and boldly declaring the truth about
the not-so-pleasant consequences looming ahead in their future.
Only repentance could stop God's judgment. The more he

preached, the more he was rejected. In the twentieth chapter of the book written by Jeremiah, he mentions that the chief officer of the Temple finally got so enraged by his preaching that he had Jeremiah's hands, feet and neck firmly secured in a torturous device called stocks and ordered that forty lashes smite his back without mercy.

All this "unfair" treatment caused Jeremiah to shamelessly complain to the Lord by saying, "You are stronger than I am and you have overpowered me. Everyone makes fun of me; they laugh at me all day long. Lord, I am ridiculed and scorned all the time because I proclaimed your message. Why was I born? Was it only to have trouble and sorrow, to end my life in disgrace?"

I cannot bring myself to criticize Jeremiah as I hear the biting sarcasm in his words. God seemed to be unaware of his plight. Jeremiah had been a faithful servant without due protection and security. You see, I too, have come to the place where I lost my spit and vinegar. Like Jeremiah, I have said, "I will forget the Lord and will no longer speak His name."

I never thought it could happen to me. If you had been on hand to speak with me after my graduation from Bible school, you would have heard nothing but confident statements regarding my assurance of God's presence and power in my life. Full of vitality and enthusiasm, I never would have dreamed that there could come a time in my life when I would want to lie down and die. The concept was foreign to me.

After seven years of full-time Christian service, I entered into a dry period of eight to ten months, experiencing no warm fuzzy feelings. Some people call it a wilderness experience. As a pastor, husband and father, I had enjoyed a string of successes; you know, the resumé/obituary-type stuff: I had hosted regular radio and television talk shows, planted three healthy churches, enjoyed six years of marriage to my precious wife and three years of being a proud papa, traveled to and preached in seven foreign countries, and had successfully ministered to a number of professional athletes.

Suddenly, at a time when everything seemed to be better than ever, a cloud of despair enveloped me as various people began to quietly criticize my leadership and many left my congregation with lame excuses. I was devastated. I didn't know what to do.

I couldn't sense God's presence in my life. My prayer life became virtually non-existent. At best, reading the Bible was tantamount to chewing shredded cardboard. Somehow, I was able to preach when necessary, but even that was a hollow experience. I felt like a fraud, giving advice, teaching, smiling, and joking on the outside, but empty on the inside. There were times when I sat at my desk for hours doing absolutely nothing. As a workaholic, these unproductive hours bombarded me with extreme guilt. But there I sat confused, angry, hurt, and tired — tired of dealing with people, tired of the pain, tired of feeling miserable.

I felt vulnerable. I was struggling. Here I was, smack-dab in the middle of a midnight trial. Thoughts crossed my mind; thoughts I had never before encountered to such a degree: "God is not 'fair.' He disapproves of me and my performance. I must have done something to deserve this. He is out to get me." Theologically, I knew that the content of those thoughts could not be substantiated, but I began to brood over them.

A root of bitterness began to spread out within my heart as circumstances worsened. I intensified my awareness of the "unfairness" of the events surrounding my life and collected data that would justify my increasingly distorted way of thinking. My desire to fight the good fight regardless of the circumstances was slowly but surely being replaced by the desire for a conflict-free environment at any price. I came to the point where I was willing to sell my spit and vinegar for quietness and security, something that I had claimed in my earlier years would never happen. I had maintained that I would never be a "spineless jellyfish."

I cried out to the Lord, "What have I done to deserve all this? I've been faithful to you all these years. I've resisted temptation and to the best of my knowledge, have walked honorably before you."

When my caring wife, Laurie, asked if there was anything she could do or say that could help, I withdrew into my shell, saying, "Naw, everything's going to work out. I'm OK. Don't worry about me." My communication level with Laurie dipped dangerously low as I continued to back away from her offered assistance.

Then, one day, I remembered a real-life story that helped me focus clearly and regain my spit and vinegar. I decided it was time to fight back against the gloominess of my "unfair" situation.

It was a crisp evening in Chicago. As they walked briskly from the restaurant, Jeffrey's wife drew closer to him. She was glad to see him after visiting relatives for a week. Earlier, he had picked her up at the bus station and had surprised her by taking her to a fine restaurant for a leisurely dinner. A few more blocks and they'd be heading for home. As they rounded the final corner they froze as, without warning, two youths jumped out from a darkened alley no more than ten yards in front of them.

With switchblades drawn, the youths advanced. "Hey man, give us all your money or we'll cut you to pieces," they said derisively.

Jeffrey instantly knew what to do. His whole body tensed and then he released a coordinated flurry of hand and feet movement. Within a matter of seconds, both would-be muggers were painfully writhing on the ground. Quickly Jeffrey and Helena ran for their car and they sped off with squealing tires.

As I remembered this account, one principle stuck with me. *The sweat of discipline and the hard work of repetition always precedes the thrill of spontaneity in any pursuit of life.* Jeffrey, my friend, had no time to think and plan his course of action when the youths approached. Although he was a martial arts instructor, he had never before been faced with a life-threatening event such as this one. His instant performance of precise body movements, however, had been preceded by years of hard work. He had virtually punished his body into shape by repeatedly practicing, to the point of exhaustion, certain moves until those moves became a part of his automatic reflexes. Under pressure, he didn't panic. Instead he acted instinctively and lived to tell the story, a little older and a little wiser. In a flash, he was able to reap the benefit of years of preparation.

As I sat at my desk that particular afternoon, reviewing my life and recalling this event in Jeffrey's life, the same old thoughts of gloom and doom began to pervade my mind. I got mad and actually said out loud, "Freeman, this is ridiculous! It's time to stop this foolishness and grow up. You've got enough dynamite of the gospel and power of the Word of God to reduce the D.P.S.I (Demons Per Square Inch) level to zero!"

Instantly, I knew where the poisonous thoughts had come from. They'd been incubated in hell. The Holy Spirit reminded me of the Scripture passage that claims that God's thoughts toward me are thoughts of peace and not evil, to give me an expected end (Jeremiah 29:11). I also knew that the frenzy of self-pity I had whipped myself into didn't correspond with the benefits of my salvation mentioned in the Bible. Instead of buying into the former thoughts, I determined to retaliate with a vengeance.

I guess you could say that I used "mental judo" or "spiritual karate," because without a moment's notice, I whirled into action using the Word of God — a blur of precise mental energy. CRACK! POW! BLAM! ZOW! The demons who were sent on a search-and-destroy mission had to flee for cover as I confronted them with many of the "It is writtens" of the Word of God. Using the Scriptures, I confronted the kingdom of darkness with the blood of Jesus, reminding Satan about my standing with Christ as a child of the King of kings and Lord of lords. Along with Paul, I proclaimed, "I am what I am by the grace of God." Along with Jeremiah, I said finally to God, "Your message is like a fire burning deep within me. I try my best to hold it in, but can no longer keep it back."

Exciting? Absolutely! It was fun being a winner — a more-than conqueror! After all, I had already read the back of the Book (the Bible) and had discovered that I had joined the winning team.

As days passed, I began to research diligently what the Bible taught about specific subjects like how to handle fear, anger, and discouragement.

During my life up to this point, I had been gripped by an inordinate need for approval from others. My whole emotional well-being depended upon my perception of the visual and verbal clues that were offered by people around me, communicated in my direction. Personal insecurity and fear had tortured me much of the time, with varying degrees of intensity. In fact, after preaching most messages, I would analyze their continuity and try to perceive their effectiveness, usually feeling I could have done much better.

It was therefore no surprise that intensified criticism from some in my congregation hit me in the solar plexus and had such a devastating negative effect on my emotions. At that time I didn't define it as such, but later on I realized I had thought that everyone should appreciate and understand me. It was this distorted way of thinking that caused such suffering within and made me vulnerable to emotional blackmail from others. Guilt trips forced me to a high level of consistent work performance, trying to win the favor of people in my sphere of influence. My life view was the perfect set-up for me to blame God, saying, "You're not 'fair,'" when circumstances became unpleasant.

I had memorized enough of the Scriptures and knew enough theology to sink a battleship, but now something was different. At this juncture in my life, I felt like Daniel did when he said, "I had no strength left . . . I was helpless" (Daniel 10:7-19). I felt like Jacob (Genesis 32), limping about because of being touched by God at the point of natural strength. Somehow, Jesus was present, waiting for me to cease trying to work for Him and begin to know Him as my Life, allowing Him to be my All in all.

Little by little, I began to get my spit and vinegar back by filling the rooms of my soul with the Word in the precise categories where I needed the most assistance. I was determined that when (not if) I got into a boxing match with the devil again, he might win the round, but he would never win the decision.

I was intoxicated with my new-found love for Jesus and His Word. Then the tests began to come. Was this a passing fancy or was this to be an established way of being for the rest of my life?

One morning, I went to visit a pastor in a neighboring town. He and his congregation had purchased a huge school facility, dirt cheap from the county, for their ministry. It had been only months prior that our congregation had lost out on a similar bid for a school facility in our community. He took me on a grand tour of their marvelous provision.

Internally, I began to think nasty, jealous thoughts motivated by the insecurity of comparing the growth of my church with his. Inwardly I was saying, "It's not 'fair.' He's been pastoring for a much shorter time than I have been pastoring and he didn't even go to Bible school." Outwardly I was exclaiming, "Praise the Lord. This building is tremendous."

Instead of entertaining those negative, critical thoughts, right there I began to employ verses that taught me to rejoice with other members of Christ's body when they rejoiced and get excited when they get blessed (Romans 12:15; 1 Corinthians 12:12-25). As I quietly meditated on these verses while touring the property, I repented to God for my lousy frame of mind, opening my heart to God's love and closing it to fleshly pettiness. An hour later, I walked to my vehicle with a spring in my step, got in and praised God for the practical lesson I had just encountered. "Mental Judo" was working. I still had my spit and vinegar!

The following Sunday I stood up to preach. I was well-prepared, but felt dry. In fact I felt kind of crabby. Maybe it was because my three-year-old son, David, had drooled toothpaste on my nicest suit earlier that morning as I assisted him with his daily grooming. Or maybe it was because I ran late all morning as the result of a long-winded telephone caller. I can't put my finger on it, but all I know is that I didn't feel too spiritual.

I preached. Oh, yes, I preached. Then I shook hands with people at the door, played briefly with some kids, picked up a crumpled bulletin, threw it away, talked seriously with a needy person, set up a counseling appointment, joked around with some teenagers, gathered the family, and finally got in the car to drive home. As soon as the car doors shut, I looked at my wife and asked, "Laurie, was the message cohesive? Was it effective?" Without waiting, I added, "I think the message bombed this morning." She tried gallantly to hide the pained, here-we-go-again expression on her face and attempted to encourage me by stating, "Oh, no, honey, the message was good. Believe me. It was good."

Upon arrival back home I went to my office and allowed the Word of God to penetrate my heart (2 Timothy 4:2; 1 Corinthians 1:26-31). I fought against the former way of thinking and literally enjoyed the rest of the day. As an added bonus, a man called later that afternoon and said, "Pastor Freeman, I just wanted you to know that your message this morning has been a blessing to my heart all day. Thank you for preaching the truth." God used me by His grace in spite of my attitude. But what was even more exciting was that I was fighting back, seeing progress and growth right before my eyes!

In a similar manner, I allowed the Holy Spirit to expose with clarity other root issues that had been coddled and embraced for years. For instance, the low communication level with my wife when I feel discouraged. I began to learn that she was my best asset — my best friend, regardless of the situation. Also, my inclination to avoid conflict when people "unfairly" criticized me for a legitimate decision made by me. I set my will to love them while holding tenaciously to my original choice. Specific study in the Word helped direct my heart into a wholesome state.

I decided that the only way to experience mental and emotional health was to plan purposely to develop God's perspective regarding the details of life. Then and only then could I break the old patterns of automatic reaction and enter into a whole new way of dealing with Satan and his crafty cohorts. I was learning how to fight spiritual battles with godly strategy, realizing it was a process I'd never outgrow.

Fight back! That is the theme of adventuresome risk takers — people who know where they have come from and where they are going. They recognize the realities of the satanic conflict. They understand that Satan thrives upon taking advantage of spiritually exposed people. They have personally experienced the devastating effects of self-pity and have decided to mount a ruthless counter-attack with the offensive weaponry of the Word. In the same way that Jeffrey painstakingly rehearsed certain physical procedures in the martial arts, we must also carefully concentrate in the spiritual realm upon the Bible and its holy principles.

We must diligently study and meditate upon specific Scriptures as the price we pay to have disciplined minds. This means we are to fill our souls with a catalog of major categories and themes.

For instance, if the diabolical one strikes with doubts regarding God's covenant of love and grace toward us, or causes anxiety about God's will in our lives, or raises questions about our eternal salvation, the Holy Spirit immediately reminds us of the needed verses and quickens us with supernatural power. With our wills, aided by the Holy Spirit's reminder, we choose to live by those verses and Satan is promptly dealt a fatal blow by frail sinners saved by grace. Instead of moping about the "unfairness" of life, we decide to channel our energies into productive thinking that honors and glorifies Jesus Christ.

There is a pertinent Scripture to neutralize every mental-attitude sin. Fear is removed by the verse that "if God is for us, who can be against us?" (Romans 8:31). Arrogance and self-righteousness are dispelled when we remember that we are not appointed to judge other people (Matthew 7:1-2; Luke 6:37; Romans 2:1). Vindictiveness and revenge are excluded by taking God at His word when He says, "Vengeance is mine; I will repay" (Romans 12:19). And we are left with no cause for jealousy or envy since our own blessings are sufficient and perfectly timed for our greatest good. We must concentrate on what we have, not on what we have not (Matthew 6:25-34).

The "fairness" issue is a particularly deceptive one because it is one of the major tactics Satan uses to cause us to lose our spit and vinegar in our most unguarded, vulnerable mo-

ments. Biblical themes such as the reality of heaven and hell,
God's patience and mercy, or our call to be ambassadors for
the King here on earth are just a few of the many categories
that are especially helpful when we are feeling despondent
because of our "unfair" circumstances.

Therefore, it is suggested that we employ the discipline
and hard work required in studying these and other categories
until they become a part of our automatic reflexes. (That is
why the appendix section is included in this book.) Satan can
intimidate sincere Christians who are fuzzy in their thinking
with regard to the Word of God. If you've lost your spit and
vinegar and seem to be trapped in a pit of despair, there is hope.

At the cross, Jesus Christ won the greatest battle ever
fought and has graciously included you and me in that victory.
A conqueror has the victory march *after* he has won the battle,
but a more-than conqueror has the victory celebration *before*
he goes to war. Christ has made us more than conquerors.
Which, when translated, means that we never have to entertain
fear about the future. Regardless what happens in the future,
we can boldly live in a victorious frame of mind, even when
confronted with heartache that causes us to weep, mourn or
grieve like never before.

This reminds me of Ruth, a woman in her late fifties.
For months I had been counseling with her periodically and
at a particularly rough time in her life she said, "I pity women
with good marriages." Her quiet statement had taken me by
surprise, especially since I knew many of the details of her
marriage of thirty-five years to a domineering man who ruled
the house with intimidating words and psychological games.

When I asked for clarification, she replied, "My marriage
has caused me to get to know the Lord like nothing else
could. Without Him, I would have left the marriage a long
time ago. And as you know, I've had my bags packed on many
occasions," she added, with a twinkle in her eyes.

"Several years ago," she continued, "I made the conscious
decision to stop taking my martyr pills and to start loving
God's Word. Everything in my situation looked terrible, but
God's presence became sweeter and sweeter. I know me. A
good marriage would have permitted me to get soft and
complacent in terms of my relationship with Jesus. As I look
back on my life, I wouldn't trade places with anybody!"

Nothing here on this planet earth — no sudden tragedy
or long-standing suffering — can rob us of our spit and vinegar.

We may lose heart for a season, but joy always is ushered in with a brand-spanking-new phase of maturity in Christ. Our goal is to grow to be like Jesus, never questioning God's plan — always trusting Him spontaneously. Remember, the sweat of discipline and hard work of repetition always precedes the thrill of spontaneity in any pursuit of life.

Did great men like Jonah or Elijah or Job ever lose their spit and vinegar? Let's peek into actual counseling sessions God had with these three men who were hurting so badly at the time that they were each on the verge of suicide.

DISCUSSION GUIDE

1. Have you ever lost your spit and vinegar? If so, try to think of that time.

2. How did that wilderness experience help to make you what you are today?

3. Select four verses of Scripture that can be applied to a current challenge in your life.

4. Write the verses on 3 x 5 cards and tape them on the four corners of your bathroom mirror. Read them whenever you see them and ask the Holy Spirit to bring them to your remembrance during each day.

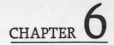

CHAPTER 6

The
Great Psychiatrist

*We may not be responsible for all the things
that happen to us, but we are responsible for the
way we behave when they do happen.*

Ralph Waldo Emerson

How would you like to have a counseling session
with God? Wouldn't that be wonderful? The next time you
feel downright crabby you could call Him. He would appear,
and you could lie on your "grouch couch" and gripe about the
terrible condition of your life. (Eat your heart out, Sigmund
Freud.) Would you care to set up an appointment for next
Thursday afternoon? Before you enthusiastically answer the
initial question, let's review some of what we know about God
and His justice:

1. God is objective and impartial. He refuses
   to be manipulated by human reasoning.
2. God sees the motives of the human heart.
   One may fool some of the people some of
   the time, but absolutely no one can pull
   the wool over His eyes at any time.
3. God is holy; therefore, He is more interested

in personal holiness than in personal happiness.
4. God emphasizes personal responsibility for
behavior. He will not spare us until we see
the wickedness of our hearts. Then, He
will not stop until we see the power of
His grace.
5. God has been known to allow certain
people to be stoned, sawn asunder, and
tormented to death, without any evidence
of success in their lives (Hebrews 11:36-39).
6. Our ideas are not always in harmony with
His.
7. God is compassionate and merciful. He
knows how much pain we can take.

Before going too much further, let's see what happens
when three people actually had counseling sessions with God
in His roving office. Don't forget, these people were hurting
emotionally. They were grumpy because they could not control
the "unfair" events in their lives. In fact, each one was so
distraught that he was seriously toying with that fatal urge —
suicide.

The first session was held on a hill overlooking the
ancient city, Nineveh, the capitol of the despised Assyrian
Empire. Jonah — the proudest, brattiest prophet in the Bible —
was in a foul frame of mind. From his vantage point on the
hill, he could see well over the walls that ran eighty miles
around the extreme outer perimeter of the city. In fact, he
observed the five walls and three moats that protected the
people of the much smaller inner city that was only three
miles long and one and a half miles wide.

The glare of the sun bore down from a cloudless sky.
Just hours before, Jonah had perspired his way up the hill,
pausing only to glance periodically over his shoulder at Nineveh.
It hadn't taken him long to find an inviting rock on which
he could rest his weary bones. As his gaze locked into the
stone walls of Nineveh, his mind raced. He had a lot to think
about.

Some years earlier, as a political representative of Israel,
he had negotiated the return of Israel's lost coastal region. He
held a deep, patriotic love for his country. His problems,
however, had begun when God had commanded him to preach

a message of repentance to the arrogant, ruthless Assyrians who were threatening to conquer his beloved nation with their dread military machine. He wasn't about to betray his own people. What if God extended kindness to the enemy because of his message? He had been repulsed at the mere thought and had fled in the opposite direction.

He squinted his eyes as he thought about the events of recent weeks. Who back home would ever believe his story? A storm at sea? Getting thrown overboard to be promptly swallowed by a huge fish for three days? Being vomited up by the fish and landing on a sandy beach, looking like a bleached alien from another planet? Preaching to his brutal enemies and then watching them repent by the thousands? The worst thing, though, was that God forgave the entire city and showed mercy to this nation that had oppressed His people for years. They deserved total destruction. Was this "fair"?

His thoughts became more and more volatile. "Well, God," he whispered irritably, "I'm waiting. Any moment now, you can wipe 'em off the map." The moments, however, became minutes. The minutes, hours. Perspiration dripped from his forehead. His eyes never wavered from the city, fully expecting fiery judgment to erupt from within its walls.

Finally, out of helpless frustration he bellowed, "God, if You're not going to destroy Nineveh, then I want to die. Go ahead, take my life!"

Jonah's desperate plea was met with silence. Then, the all-knowing all-powerful God of the universe spoke, asking one penetrating question, pregnant with meaning: "Jonah, what right do you have to be angry?"

It sounded like an elementary question, but it cut down to the root of Jonah's selfishness. God didn't stop there, though. According to Jonah 4, He proceeded to give Jonah a kindergarten object lesson. God caused a large castor oil plant to grow miraculously directly behind him. The resultant shade produced a mood swing in Jonah, from deep depression to exceeding joy. For the remainder of the day, Jonah basked in the cool shadow of the plant, happy as a window salesman in a hurricane.

The next morning, however, a worm attacked the plant and it died just as quickly as it had grown. A scorching east wind blew in with suffocating heat, causing Jonah's mood to swing back to total despair.

After Jonah expressed his second death wish, God confronted the absurdity of Jonah's spiritual apathy toward the welfare of the people of Nineveh. Jonah's primary concern was with his own physical comfort, yet he lacked compassion for the 120,000 little children in Nineveh. Through it all, God exposed Jonah's deep-seated hatred for His mercies and his inordinate preoccupation with his own ego needs.

God used a plant, a worm, the sun, and a hot summer wind to get His point across. Do you think God used a strange counseling technique? Wait till you see His approach with Elijah!

The second counseling session was in a cave. In 1 Kings 19, Elijah had prayed a twenty-eight-second prayer, and fire had come down from heaven. After that tremendous victory, Jezebel had scared the living daylights out of Elijah and he ran almost one hundred miles from Mount Carmel to Beersheba. Needless to say, he was frightened!

Then he ran into the wilderness, plopped himself down under a juniper tree, and wanted to die. To make a long story short, he ultimately ended up in a cave in the mountainside. As he sat there, a strong wind, an earthquake, and a fire occurred in front of him, in that order.

Finally, Elijah heard a still, small voice. No one knows what was said. Then the Lord spoke audibly with this incisive question: "What are you doing here, Elijah?" The prophet didn't respond verbally, but he acted quickly because the next thing we read is that he took off for Damascus to anoint someone as king.

Thus far, God has been light on words, but heavy with action. How do you think He handled His next client?

The third session was held in the ashes of a burned-out home. Job had lost hope. He felt forsaken by a God who had used him for a "whipping boy." He thought God had left him to work things out on his own. At one point, he arrogantly said that if he ever found God's throne, his mouth would be filled with arguments. He had lost virtually everything. His three friends were slowly but surely tearing down what little self-esteem he had left.

How would you handle an intense counseling case such as this one? Let's step aside and watch the Great Psychiatrist at work.

In Job 38:3, God bluntly commanded, "Stand up now like a man and answer the questions I ask you." During the next two chapters God dazzled Job with fancy footwork. He pulled back the curtains and revealed the incredible power behind nature.

He showed Job the very foundations of the earth; what kept the sea from covering the entire face of the earth; the beginnings of ice and frost; the exact place where light came forth to shine upon the world; the innumerable stars and galaxies stretching across space; the miraculous beginnings of each morning; the laws of precipitation, evaporation and condensation; the intrigues of the deep sea; the cause of lightning, thunder and clouds; the intricacies of the animal kingdom; and the perfect harmony of the earth, nature and the entire universe, from the macro to the micro.

At this point, Job gasped for breath and blurted out, "Behold, I am vile, what shall I answer Thee? I will lay my hand upon my mouth." Instead of getting more depressed, Job began to think, "If God is that powerful — if He is that great — is He not big enough to take care of my problems? I am persuaded that He can take care of me."

The "fairness" issue was not specifically addressed by God. No camels were raised from the dead. No homes were rebuilt. No children were resurrected. No prayers were dramatically answered. Not one miracle happened — just a childlike trust in God's great authority!

Job stopped justifying himself. Absolutely nothing changed in his environment. The only thing that changed was his attitude toward God. He no longer thought of God as a cruel taskmaster. He saw God as one who was bigger than all his questions about "fairness."

While Jonah never seemed to respond positively, Elijah went from his counseling session with God as a changed man. He no longer was a sniveling crybaby!

God exhibited a rather unique counseling technique with all three men. He was extremely patient, allowing them to function irrationally without instant reprimand. The therapeutic relationships were fostered by His unconditional love for them. He waited for the appropriate moments and then challenged each man with the brutal facts.

The casual observer may decide that God's counseling style was rather abrupt, perhaps unfeeling — even "unfair." However, from our grandstand seats in the 20th century we can see with 20/20 hindsight that His absolute justice and mercy blended together in perfect counsel — specifically directed to the *real* needs rather than the *perceived* needs of each one.

Now, how would you like to have a personal counseling session with God the next time you are adamant about your right to know the answers to all the "why" questions in your life? Do you think you would impudently demand your rights? How about tomorrow? We can schedule an appointment — perhaps at 3:30 in the afternoon?

DISCUSSION GUIDE

1. If you could have anything, what would you ask of God? See 1 Kings 3:9.

2. Think for a moment: What trials in your life might God be using to turn your attention to Him?

3. In light of what you know and have read about the attributes of God, what would His counsel be to you right now?

CHAPTER 7

Hey,
God's Got Rights,
Too!

*Nothing influences the quality of our life more
than how we respond to trouble.*
                                        Erwin G. Tieman

Have you ever been a red-faced, irate consumer?
Have you ever felt ripped off by the manufacturer of a product?
How about the corduroy pants that shrank two sizes after the
first wash? How about the "lemon" car that was too young to
smoke?

Some people are too embarrassed to complain about a
bad transaction. But most people have no qualms about making
a scene because they believe in the old adage, "The squeaky
wheel gets the grease."

I'll never forget the man I saw at a car dealership a
number of years ago. He was in the process of raking the sales
manager over the coals for selling him a lemon. The flustered
general manager was present, trying to bring a sense of order
to the whole situation. No matter how hard he tried, he could
not quiet the man who was boisterously yelling, "Even if I
have to stay overnight, I will stand right here until you give
me a new car or give my money back! I'm sick and tired of the

lousy hunk of metal you sold me! I've got my rights!"

Some of us can identify with that man, especially those of us who have had similar experiences. We can also understand the rights of the victims of crime, overtaxed citizens, battered wives, unborn children, and prisoners of war. In fact, there is a whole list of special interest groups that have points to make for legitimate cases:

Women's rights	Men's rights
Criminal rights	Animal rights
Patient rights	Human rights
Constitutional rights	States' rights
Labor rights	Religious rights
Civil rights	Consumer rights

Each of these has a degree of legitimacy, but where do we stop? Do we give mothers a right to decide whether they want their unborn children to live? Do we slap a murderer on the wrist because his lawyer successfully argues "temporary insanity"? Do we excuse a high school boy for raping a girl because the judge feels that the boy had been subjected to sexual stimuli in society and was only doing what was natural? Do we make it legal to kill millions of unborn children while bringing harsh fines and swift imprisonment for killing bald eagles? Do we adopt the philosophy that personal rights and pleasure are more important than loyalty to marriage vows? Do we continue to allow confessed criminals to escape the consequences of their actions because of foolish technicalities?

At this moment I can hear a sweet, little old lady in the background yelling at the top of her lungs, "Stop asking so many questions. You're depressing me!" Whew, I'm glad she interrupted me, because we must pause and give equal time to another set of rights that are rarely considered in the midst of all the hub-bub.

What about God's rights? Have you ever stopped to think about it? He has allowed himself to be victimized. Over the course of history many have exploited His name for personal gain. He has been hated without cause, slandered without reason, and forgotten without apology. His character has been misrepresented when humans have suffered. His name has been cursed when humans have reaped the results of personal sin. His family has been abused and injured by every kind of irresponsible behavior. At best, His authority has been ignored.

He has been blamed for famine, war, and disease. People have killed other people in His name. His wisdom has been mocked by each successive generation. His standards of holiness have always been considered old-fashioned by the sin-soaked society of every era.

Is He big enough to handle all this abuse? Of course He is. He is not insecure. He can take care of Himself. But the point is that because of His unconditional love, He has chosen to make himself vulnerable. He is wide open to abuse from humans who are especially interested in their own private rights.

In fact, if we want to magnify the "fairness" issue and demand our rights, we'd better be thankful that He doesn't take us up on our requests. Let's face it — we all deserve hell and damnation. There's not an obedient bone or tissue in our bodies. Our hearts are deceitful and desperately wicked. We couldn't objectively determine the proper standard for our rights, even if we tried.

It always amazes me whenever I think of what God could demand of us. He could demand a perfect human response from us at all times without giving us second chances. He has the right to dispense the quick judgment that mankind deserves.

Instead, He has designed a new plan: "Operation Mercy." Even while His rights have been blatantly violated all across this planet, His mercies have not been affected. The rain still falls on the just and the unjust alike. His mercies are new and fresh every morning. One of the mysteries of God is His patience with indifferent humans.

God made us. He also created the world. Therefore, He has the perfect right to be listened to and thanked, even in the midst of pain and suffering. He deserves the right to be loved and respected above any relationship, material possession, or pursuit of life.

It warms and encourages my heart every time I think of Jan. It was just one month ago that I attended her funeral. At the age of twenty-nine she graduated into the glorious presence of Jesus after suffering most of her life from a serious heart and lung condition.

Her primary motivation in life was to honor God's right to be trusted. Even in the midst of her continual pain and uncertainty, she praised His name. Her entire schedule was filled with an all-consuming drive to minister to others beyond the limits of her own four walls. With her husband, Randy, she did so through prayer, telephone calls and notes of love.

Oh, sure, she had her times of questions, negativity and doubts, but she always came through with a greater determination to amplify God's rights above her own. Jan's life has left a legacy of love and a heritage of hope to the many people who were the recipients of her thoughtfulness.

We, like Jan, must carefully protect His right to be worshiped and served above all others regardless of our circumstances. Great blessings are heaped upon those who honor His right to be trusted, even in the midst of heart-rending trials of faith.

If God's rights were honored and guarded, almost every other human right that demands instant attention would be non-existent. "Fairness" would no longer be the issue that energizes so many causes. Wounded individuals would submit to God's Word instead of wallowing in self-pity.

DISCUSSION GUIDE

1. Over the past year, in what ways have you honored God's rights?

2. How can you sharpen your spiritual focus on Him who is invisible?

3. Meditate for a few minutes on the mystery of God's patience toward you. Think of a recent time when you behaved like an impudent brat. Thank Him for His longsuffering with you.

4. How will you try to respond to Him the next time He allows a trial to come your way?

CHAPTER 8

Wounded Crybabies

Our suffering is not worthy of the name of suffering. When I consider my crosses, tribulations, and temptations; I shame myself almost to death, thinking what are they in comparison of the sufferings of my blessed Savior Christ Jesus.
                                        Martin Luther

Crybabies. Crybabies. They are everywhere. They have been spotted in restaurants. They have been sighted in bars. They have been seen whimpering in church pews. They have been recognized in hospitals and educational institutions. They also have been discovered on the mission field.

They all share one common denominator — they strongly feel that life has dealt them a dirty deal. Don't ask them how they are feeling unless you are prepared to hear a juicy "war story," complete with the latest gossip. They will bend your ear for hours if you let them. Wide-eyed, they will dramatize the details in a sentimental tone. In fact, you will be tempted to give them an Oscar for their performance.

In 1 Corinthians 11:18-19, Paul said that at times there are factions and divisions present in a local church, so that those who are genuine can be plainly recognized. Motivated by love, as the Head of the church, Jesus Christ allows crises to develop in a local assembly of believers. Before long a few professional crybabies start reacting against the pastor and ultimately gripe about how "unfair" the church policies are. Eventually they influence a number of namby-pamby cowards to grumble with them.

Little do they realize that God reserves the right to test the hearts of His people. He will use other human beings, uncontrollable events, unexpected circumstances, the piercing of the Word, and the conviction of the Holy Spirit to reveal how well they have applied what they have heard.

It reminds me of the bunch of wounded crybabies who were disgruntled about receiving equal pay for unequal work. Let's take a break and read this classic story and decipher some of the underlying issues:

> For the kingdom of heaven is like a landowner who went out early in the morning [around 6 A.M.] to hire men to work in his vineyard. He agreed to pay them a denarius [penny] for the day and sent them into his vineyard.
>
> About the third hour [9 A.M.] he went out and saw others standing in the marketplace doing nothing. He told them, "You also go and work in my vineyard, and I will pay you whatever is right." So they went.
>
> He went out again about the sixth hour [12 noon] and the ninth hour [3 P.M.] and did the same thing. About the eleventh hour [5 P.M.] he went out and found still others standing around. He asked them, "Why have you been standing here all day long doing nothing?"
>
> "Because no one has hired us," they answered.
>
> He said to them, "You also go and work in my vineyard."
>
> When the evening came around [6 P.M.], the owner of the vineyard said to his foreman, "Call the workers and pay them their wages, beginning with the last ones hired and going on to the first."
>
> The workers who were hired about the eleventh hour [5 P.M.] came and each received a denarius. So when those came who were hired first, they expected to receive more. But each one of them also received a denarius. When they received it, they began to grumble against the landowner, "These men who were hired last worked only one hour," they said. "And you have made them equal to us who have borne the burden of the work and the heat of the day" (Matthew 20:1-12, NIV).

At this point in the narrative, what are your impressions

of the poor men who started work at six o'clock in the morning? Do you feel sorry for them? Do you think they have a legal gripe against the landowner? Should they form a labor union and refuse to work until equitable standards are set for the workers? Do you believe they are making a big deal out of nothing? Are their rights important?

Before we raise too many questions, let's find out what the landowner's response was in this ticklish situation. He is addressing the biggest crybaby of the early birds. Ready?

> But he answered one of them, "Friend, I am not being unfair to you. Didn't you agree to work for a denarius? Take your pay and go. I want to give the man who was hired last the same as I gave you. Don't I have the right to do what I want with my own money? Or are you envious because I am generous?" (Matthew 20:13-15, NIV).

If we approach this case from the viewpoint of "fairness" logic, we could easily be drawn into feeling sorry for the men who worked all day. After all, it wasn't "fair" that they had to do most of the work.

Furthermore, the landowner wasn't at all sensitive to the fact that they worked during the hottest part of the day. The other fellows worked for only an hour during the coolness of the late afternoon and yet they received the same wage. But the toughest part to understand is that the landowner seemed deliberately to take delight in paying the late arrivers first and the hard-working first group last. It doesn't seem "fair"! Does it?

While this is difficult to understand from a human posture, let's change glasses and view the whole scenario from the standpoint of God's justice.

This parable is about the kingdom of heaven, where the grace and justice of God are dominant factors and the humanistic ideals of situational ethics and "fairness" logic are totally foreign.

The crux of this case is that God, pictured as a landowner in this parable, has the right to do what He wants when He wants. He can be generous with His mercy if He desires, even if some humans waste their whole lifetimes begrudging His benevolence. He has the right to expose the attitude in which work for Him is accomplished. He will exercise His right to challenge wounded crybabies with "unfair" circumstances, hoping that they'll stop griping and start growing. He classifies all work in His kingdom as being on the same level.

In other words, when all believers stand before Jesus, each one will receive the same wage: GRACE. It doesn't matter whether one person was a missionary who suffered great hardships for fifty years in a remote land, or another individual lived like the devil all his life and then had a deathbed conversion. Each person will be in heaven even though he didn't deserve it and could not have earned it if he tried.

When Jesus says, "Take up your cross and follow Me, even if you don't understand a thing," we tend to say, "OK, but what will I get in return?" When life deals us a rotten hand, we are inclined to whimper and nurse a foul attitude against God.

We usually follow Jesus on the basis of what we receive as a benefit. Wasn't that Satan's prime accusation against Job? Instead, Jesus desires that we serve Him regardless of the results. We learn, like the laborers, to experience the joy of working for Him in our particular vineyard, trusting Him to reward us on the basis of His justice.

When we behave like the first bunch of sour-grape workers, it is usually because God is meddling in our previously untouched territory. He patiently waits for the precise timing and then challenges us with a brand-new test after providing us with a supply of His power. If we reject His provision, we become wounded crybabies, evoking sympathy from empty-headed observers. But God sees through the smokescreen and continues to probe until we yield to His plan in sweet surrender.

It was with great interest that I recently read how Victor Frankl, the famous Jewish psychiatrist and father of logotherapy, suffered three grim years at Auschwitz and other Nazi prisons. During this time, he watched many people blame their environment, lose all hope and commit suicide; while others remained strong and actually thrived under the same conditions. His afterthought about prison camp went like this:

> Life in a concentration camp tore open the human soul and exposed its depths. Is it surprising that in those depths we again found only human qualities which in their very nature were a mixture of good and evil? The rift dividing good from evil, which goes through all human beings, reaches into the lowest depths and becomes apparent even on the bottom of the abyss which is laid open by the concentration camp.[1]

Frankl felt that any attempt to restore a person's inner

strength in the camp had first to succeed in showing him or
her some future goals. At this point, he is fond of quoting
Nietzsche's words, "He who has a *why* to live for can bear
with almost any *how*."[2] Read carefully as Frankl goes on to
share the attitudes that kept him sane in a most "unfair"
environment:

> Once the meaning of suffering had been revealed to
> us, we refused to minimize or alleviate the camp's tortures
> by ignoring them or harboring false illusions and enter-
> taining artificial optimism. Suffering had become a task
> on which we did not want to turn our backs. We had
> realized its hidden opportunities for achievement, the
> opportunities which caused the poet Rilke to write, *"Wie
> viel ist aufzuleiden!"* (How much suffering there is to get
> through!) Rilke spoke of "getting through suffering" as
> others would talk of "getting through work." There was
> plenty of suffering for us to get through. Therefore, it
> was necessary to face up to the full amount of suffering,
> trying to keep moments of weakness and furtive tears
> to a minimum. But there was no need to be ashamed
> of tears, for tears bore witness that man had the greatest
> of courage, the courage to suffer. Only very few realized
> that.[3]

Frankl has well observed that as human beings, we rarely
enjoy the luxury of selecting our circumstances, but we can
always choose our attitudes in spite of the circumstances. And
may I add, our attitude toward God is *always* the ultimate
issue in *every* wound.

Sabina Wurmbrand also endured a prison camp experience
in Romania. Capture her attitude as you read an account from
her book, *The Pastor's Wife:*

> Next morning a guard came and told me to pack. The
> same day I was sent back to the labor colonies. This
> time it was a State pig farm, where fifty women tended
> several hundred swine. The years had been hard, but
> this was the hardest of all. Food was at starvation level.
> We dragged ourselves from our beds at 5:00 A.M., still
> wearing the filthy rags in which we had laid down, and
> went out into the cold and darkness to feed the pigs.
> The sties were ankle-deep in liquid filth — the one sub-
> stance that never froze. A vile, nauseating stench hung
> over the place and penetrated every angle of our huts.

It hung about the body and hair. The very skilly we
slopped up with our wooden spoons savored of it. We
were better off than the prodigal son: we filled our bellies
with the husks that the swine did eat.
The meaning fell away from things. Death stared me
in the face. The whole world was made of tears and
despair as never before and a cry rose from my heart:
"My God, my God, why hast Thou forsaken me?"
Trying to clean their sties was as hopeless as trying
to clean the world. Each day we started afresh, hungry
and half-dead, to cart away in barrows the mountains
of filth. I knew there was no hope for me, nor the world,
and expected only to die.
And, perhaps, in a psychological condition as this, I
should not have survived for long. But happily it did not
last for many weeks. I am convinced that the Lord heard
my prayers and took me out according to His plan. I
had only to learn a very deep lesson, to drink the cup
to its bitterest dregs; and now I am thankful that I
passed through this hard school, which teaches you the
highest love, love towards God, even when He gives you
nothing but suffering.[4]

Sabina learned a valuable lesson while enduring this
horrifying existence. She learned to love and trust Him even
in the midst of pain. She served Him, enjoying a peace even
though she didn't understand the "whys" of her environment.

We, however, do not need to be placed in a concentration
camp to glean this same principle. Life offers many classroom
settings that assist us in learning to serve God regardless of
the visible benefits: the church choir ("Rachel gets all the solo
parts"); the job ("Herb got promoted before I did"); the hospital
("No one has been in to visit me"); or the home ("My family
doesn't appreciate all the work I do").

I have a pet theory. *I believe that the closer we get to
the administrative center of any political party, business en-
deavor, church work, or family system, the more opportunities
we have for personal disillusionment.* Does that statement
sound reasonable? Actually, it is painfully all too true.

I know that as a pastor, I have watched as new folks
have attended my church and expressed great excitement about
the music, the message, the people, and the overall atmosphere
of the church. After attending for a couple of months, they
decide to get involved in some ministry of the church. Invariably

they will approach me a few weeks later with blanched looks on their faces, saying, "Pastor, when I first came to this church, I thought it was the greatest thing since sliced bread. But after I've gotten involved, I think that this church is more like F Troop." Thank God, they are now confronted with a practical opportunity to apply Scriptural principles and to grow in the grace and knowledge of Jesus Christ!

It always saddens me when I cross paths with embittered former employees of various business institutions or disgruntled ex-members of an assortment of churches. Some are driven by a desire to destroy their former authority figures, while others, in quiet desperation, tenaciously hold on to a wounded spirit.

One thing I have noticed, though, is that each one possesses a "'fairness' fixation." They have lost sight of a great, big, wonderful God. Instead, their entire focus is on how badly they were hurt and how they are going to retaliate. Passionate prayer, soul winning, and personal Bible study all take a back seat to their preoccupation with the "unfairness" of their prior treatment.

I am not quick to judge, however, because I have been exactly where they are. Each time, I am reminded of my need to pray for them and keep my own fuss budget balanced.

DISCUSSION GUIDE

1. What or who is there in your past that you need to forgive and leave behind?

2. How do you respond when your work goes unrecognized?

3. Have you caught a glimpse of God's greatness? Bow your heart before Him and ask for a fresh vision of His greatness and power.

CHAPTER 9

How
to Balance
Your Fuss Budget

*People do not like to be put upon the grindstone,
but they are dull tools for the purposes for which
God designs to use them.*

Anonymous

Wouldn't it be fun to spend money without ever worrying about the state of your bank account? Ah, yes, it would make one feel footloose and fancy free. Not a care in the world. Just spend, spend, spend!

I recently grinned mischievously when I saw a person wearing a button that read: WHEN THE GOING GETS TOUGH, THE TOUGH GO SHOPPING. I couldn't help it. It struck me funny and I actually giggled out loud as we walked past, much to the embarrassment of my wife. Later on, after I regained my composure, I went into a deep thought about the spiritual implications of that slogan.

When the going gets tough, many people react violently and expend great amounts of mental and emotional energy with zero productivity as the net result. Their useless thinking leads to useless activity. For instance, notice how far Elijah ran in 1 Kings 19, after his tremendous victory on the top of Mount Carmel. A few hours after the Mount Carmel victory,

Jezebel told him she was going to kill him, and his mind became so filled with fear that he entered into the useless exercise of literally running almost one hundred miles to escape her wrath.

Elijah's futile expenditure of energy was almost as crazy as the activity of Adam and Eve in the Garden of Eden (Genesis 3). After they ate of the forbidden fruit, they began the foolish action of sewing fig leaves together to cover their nakedness. I have never seen a fig leaf, but I am told that, when fully grown, they are about the size of a dinner plate. And a fig leaf, when picked off the tree, shrinks to the size of a teacup within twenty-four hours. Does useless thinking lead to needless activity? Of course it does!

That's why it is important to budget the account of our minds with detailed instructions from the Word. If we don't, we will come up short when life presents us with a bill that demands immediate response.

I can speak with authority on this subject because I have allowed overspending in my fuss budget more than once in my life. Many times I have allowed my emotions to become the boss of my attitude, thereby permitting myself the right to fuss excessively when I felt that life had treated me "unfairly."

As a youngster, if a playmate called me a "dummy," I would run away mad. If my older brother, Steve, was granted a special privilege, I'd blubber about the "unfairness" of the decision. If my younger sister, Beth, got away with something that I didn't get away with at her age, I'd grumble. I expended much of my mental and emotional resources focusing on the "fairness" of my circumstances at school, at home, and on the playground. Little did I realize that progressively the fuss part of my emotional budget was developing uncontrollable spending habits.

Events culminated to the point where at the age of seventeen, I found myself arrogantly standing in the doorway of my bedroom with hands stuffed deeply in my pockets, telling my father that I hated him and everything he stood for. As circumstances became more intolerable, I decided to leave my home in Alberta, Canada, to hitchhike aimlessly around North America. On a cold wintry morning, I did just that. I stuck out my thumb with $24 in my pocket and was gone from the restrictions. Free at last! Or so I thought. If I were to locate my scrapbook and show some verbal snapshots of my adventures while on the road, they would include:

1. Trying to hitch a ride, twenty miles from civilization, in the middle of the Canadian Rocky Mountains with a road-closing snow storm brewing. (Anxious.)
2. Valiantly selling magazines in Vancouver, British Columbia, trying to make a buck. (Disillusioned.)
3. Spending almost three weeks in a juvenile prison in Portland, Oregon. (Terrified.)
4. Trying to hitch a ride for fifteen hours — stuck in Lodi, California. (Frustrated.)
5. Shoveling snow from many doorsteps in Seattle, Washington. ($58 richer.)
6. Panhandling and shoplifting in Victoria, British Columbia. (Excited.)
7. Conning a minister in Banff, Alberta. ($30 richer.)
8. Sleeping beside the road in Weed, California. (Lonely.)
9. Sitting in an evening church service as a long-haired hippie, after taking drugs and drinking beer at an afternoon party in Boothbay Harbor, Maine. (Amused.)
10. Cruising through the Sierra Nevada Mountains of California in a Kharmann-Ghia at 90 m.p.h while the owner of the car slept. (Exhilarated.)
11. Working as a baker's helper in a fancy Portland, Maine, restaurant. (Bored.)
12. Sleeping under the stars in a town park somewhere in a western province of Canada, with hippie-hating cowboys boisterously drinking beer and carousing not more than 200 feet away. (Scared.)

My personal public-relations program told everyone that I was carefree, but, on the inside, I was empty with no resources left to draw from. I was burdened down with the debt of guilt. I had built my apparent happiness upon the despair of others, namely my parents. Without realizing it, I had manipulated myself into carrying the deep root of crybabyitis.

I knew something had to change. And something did

change after my conversion to Jesus Christ on September 10, 1972, and entrance into Bible school on the very next day. I began to learn some life-changing principles that assisted me in balancing my fuss budget.

One such principle that especially helped curb the massive spending program of my emotions was *The Doctrine of All or Nothing:*

- "For *all* things are for your sakes . . ." (2 Corinthians 4:15).
- "And *all* things are of God . . ." (2 Corinthians 5:18).
- "And we know that *all* things work together for good . . ." (Romans 8:28).
- "For of Him, and through Him, and to Him are *all* things . . ." (Romans 11:36).
- "And every man that striveth for the mastery is temperate in *all* things . . ." (1 Corinthians 9:25).
- "Charity . . . beareth *all* things, believeth *all* things, hopeth *all* things, endureth *all* things" (1 Corinthians 13:7).
- ". . . the God of *all* comfort; Who comforteth us in *all* our tribulations . . ." (2 Corinthians 1:3-4).
- ". . . that ye, always having *all* sufficiency in *all* things . . ." (2 Corinthians 9:8).
- ". . . Him who worketh *all* things after the counsel of His own will" (Ephesians 1:11).
- "Do *all* things without murmurings and disputings" (Philippians 2:14).
- ". . . I count *all* things but loss . . ." (Philippians 3:8).
- "Casting *all* your care upon Him; for He careth for you" (1 Peter 5:7).
- ". . . the God of *all* grace . . ." (1 Peter 5:10).
- "And God shall wipe away *all* your tears . . ." (Revelation 21:4).

OR:

- "Let *nothing* be done through strife or vainglory . . ." (Philippians 2:3).
- "For we brought *nothing* into this world, and it is certain we can carry *nothing* out" (1 Timothy 6:7).
- "But let patience have her perfect work, that ye may be perfect [mature] and entire, wanting *nothing*" (James 1:4).

- "... for without Me you can do *nothing*" (John 15:5).
- "... and have not charity, I am *nothing*" (1 Corinthians 13:2).
- "... with God *nothing* shall be impossible" (Luke 1:37).
- "... the flesh profiteth *nothing* ..." (John 6:63).
- "Great peace have they which love Thy law [Word]: and *nothing* shall offend them" (Psalm 119:165).

As you have already noticed, each verse has either the word "all" or "nothing." The remarkable conclusion is that when the word "all" is used, it means *all*—not 99.9 percent. When the term "nothing" appears, it means just that, absolutely *nothing*. There's no room for debate, rationalization, or calculated indifference.

The uniqueness and extenuating circumstances surrounding our lots in life may cause us to view these verses with a jaundiced eye. We, however, are invited to come to terms with life's raw deals by submitting willingly to God's plan in God's way, in God's timing—hence *The Doctrine of All or Nothing*.

I discovered *The Doctrine of All or Nothing* one day quite by accident after being deeply offended by the way a Bible school classmate had "unfairly" treated me. We had traded some heated words and I retreated to my bedroom, an emotional mess. I was almost ready to settle down, nurse my grudge and plot revenge, when something inside motivated me to pick up my Bible. I don't do this often, nor do I highly recommend it, but I shut my eyes, twirled the Bible around, opened it and placed my index finger on a page, hoping it didn't say, "... and Judas ... went and hanged himself."

Much to my great surprise, my finger had pointed to the Psalm 119:165 text quoted above. I was flabbergasted! I stared at the word "nothing" and immediately began to rationalize. I tried valiantly to make it mean something else, but I couldn't. I wanted to talk myself into having a pity party, but that verse kept bombarding my heart with specific truth. I couldn't fight it and maintain an honest relationship with the Holy Spirit at the same time. Before long, I embarked on an intensive study, formulating a personal conviction regarding *The Doctrine of All or Nothing*. This conviction enabled me not only to repent for the sourpuss attitude I had harbored toward my colleague, but also to ask for and receive forgiveness for the wrongs I had committed against my parents during the rebellion of my youth.

As a result, I was able to balance my fuss budget with the inescapable light from the Word of God. When my camouflaged condition of crybabyitis started acting up because of some rat fink bugging me, I learned to rest upon the fact that *all* things were for my sake, including "unfair" treatment from human buzzards. It was then I began to learn how to trust God and experience His joy regardless of my circumstances.

DISCUSSION GUIDE

1. How are you balancing your fuss budget in light of God's Word?

2. How do you respond when God says no?

3. What are you taking for granted for which you should be expressing gratitude?

CHAPTER 10

Buzzard Bait

*To have suffered much is like knowing many
languages: It gives the sufferer access to many more
people.*

Anonymous

The desert sun was smoldering as he dragged himself through the sand. He had been in desperate straits for approximately two days without water. Everything looked the same to him as he gallantly struggled for every inch of progress. The camera zoomed in on his face, which was etched with high-level anxiety. His eyes were glazed over with bewilderment. Periodically he glanced in fear at the buzzards circling patiently in the sky above him. He knew full well what to expect if help didn't arrive. He was about to become "buzzard bait."

I shifted uneasily in my overstuffed chair as I vicariously entered into the mounting plot of an old western movie on television. During the commercial break, I began to reflect on the activity of the buzzards. Their circling behavior was reminiscent of how self-appointed advice experts behave with hurting people.

As I thought more about it, I became painfully aware of the fact that I too, possessed the propensity to think, talk, and act with that same nasty "buzzard" nature. I became increasingly conscious of my human tendency to analyze and judge others based on my preconceived notions. It didn't take long for me to realize that I, too, was in desperate need of God's wisdom.

When someone is in the perplexed state of mind of a desert experience, the last thing he needs is human "buzzards" coming over to visit him. "Buzzards" often give religiously pat, oversimplified answers to people suffering from emotional problems, answers which only serve to drive them into deeper despair and disillusionment. Consequently, the terminally ill, victims of crime, and other walking wounded tend to feel like pieces of "buzzard bait," waiting to be picked apart by well-intentioned people. The advice that "buzzards" often give reminds me of a story that David Seamands relates in his book *Healing for Damaged Emotions.*

> Perhaps you have heard about the man who was traveling on a dinner flight. When he opened his prepackaged meal, right on top of the salad he saw an enormous roach. When he got home, he wrote an indignant letter to the president of that airline. A few days later, a special delivery letter came from the president. He was all apologies. "This was very unusual, but don't worry. I want to assure you that that particular airplane has been fumigated. In fact, all the seats and upholstery have been stripped out. We have taken disciplinary action against the stewardess who served you that meal, and she may even be fired. It is highly probable that this particular aircraft will be taken out of service. I can assure you that it will never happen again. And I trust that you will continue to fly with us."
>
> Well, the man was terrifically impressed by such a letter until he noticed something. Quite by accident, the letter he had written had stuck to the back of the president's letter. When he looked at his own letter he saw a note at the bottom that said, "Reply with the regular roach letter."[1]

When people are struggling with uncontrollable, life-changing events, they are often chagrined by the wickedness of their hearts. They find themselves saying and doing desperate things. They make emotionally based decisions and are filled with confusion. The last thing on earth they need is a lecture from some "buzzard" who gives them the regular-roach-letter reply to their "fairness" questions.

Job's three friends, Bildad, Zophar, and Eliphaz, were "buzzards." They didn't have a clue as to what was happening with Job. For days they circled silently, watching his every move. Finally, Job could stand it no longer. He began to talk irrationally. He cursed the day he was born and blatantly exposed his fears. That was all those "buzzards" needed. Each took his turn to preach at this despondent man. They accused him of sin, heaping condemnation upon his bowed frame. They argued with him and badgered him until Job didn't know what to do.

In the same manner, modern day "buzzards" are attracted to vulnerable people. As "buzzards," we are uncomfortable in the presence of people who are feeling excruciating pain. When we are behaving like "buzzards," we will question other people's faith as prayers for healing are offered. Unknowingly, "buzzards" bludgeon diseased and emotionally distraught individuals with opinionated theology. These lifeless doctrines are used to destroy rather than edify.

"Buzzards" cannot rejoice when others rejoice, neither can they identify with the sorrow of others. This occurs because they have not dealt properly with the hurts in their own lives. As "buzzards," they either repress their own emotional pain for religious reasons, or they express it in other ways. Since they have maladjusted to the justice of God in their own personal experiences, they wreak havoc in the Christian community with their dogmatic, legalistic preachments.

When I graduated from Bible school, in so many words I said to the world, "Here I am, all you lucky people." The casual observer may have thought that I was exhibiting a rather arrogant attitude, but it was more of a confidence in and love for Jesus Christ than anything else. I felt enthusiasm and excitement as I looked into the future.

Along with that zeal, though, came a desperate lack of maturity. That mix was "trouble looking for a place to happen." As prime "buzzard" material, I had enough knowledge to be dangerous.

I'm not proud of the circumstances surrounding it, but I vividly remember the confused look on Sandra's face at the end of our only counseling session together. As a new, full-time pastor in a small church in Maine, I had taken her on as my first genuine counseling case. I was a bundle of nerves.

Sandra came into my tiny office and sat down in the

chair opposite the desk. Very professionally, I welcomed her
and then parroted the fine opening-a-counseling-session
technique, "Well, what brings you here at this time?"

It was all downhill from that point. As she unburdened
herself, I became increasingly worried and self conscious about
my verbal responses to her. To this day, I am thankful that
she had the gift of gab for as long as she did. But then the
inevitable happened. She stopped talking. She had finished
her story, complete with handkerchief and tears. Silence — awkward, embarrassing silence — was all that was left.

I looked at her and she at me. Her eyes seemed to be
appealing for an answer or at least some type of response.
The clock on the wall made an awfully loud ticking noise.
The tension in my emotions and in the room became unbearable.

Finally, I could stand it no longer. "Sandra," I said impulsively, "all you need to do is to trust in God. Yes, that's
it — trust in God!" I stopped and then panicked, immediately
understanding that while my counsel was theologically correct,
it was unsuitable for the moment.

Her countenance clouded with confusion and then
exploded with reaction to the inappropriateness of my response.
Without another word, she gathered her things and vacated
the premises, never to be heard from again. It all happened
so quickly.

I sat at my desk for more than an hour, overwhelmed
with feelings of inadequacy.

Upon looking back, I can clearly see my insensitive
"buzzard-like" behavior, not only in this situation, but at other
times. I didn't have sinister motives in mind. Most of my
"buzzard" approaches to situations were directly related to a
sincere desire to help, but implemented in an immature, mis-
guided fashion.

This, I think, is the root issue with most "buzzards." But,
how can those of us who have "buzzard" tendencies change?
Very simply: *We shut up!*

The only substitute for wisdom is silence. In Psalm 46:10,
David writes, "Be still [cease striving], and know that I am
God . . ." In silence, God can begin to draw "buzzards" out of
the heated production of their religious activity. Quietly, He
brings them into a balanced love for others. He causes them
to look beyond faults and gives them the ability to minister
to the true needs of others, speaking a word in season to

those who are weary. Remember, Job's three friends were doing quite well until they opened their mouths!

Someone who has adjusted properly to God's justice in the midst of deep hurt is comfortable with silence. He is sparing with advice and does not offer pious platitudes. He is not shocked when another person talks or acts desperately. He does not try to reason with or argue with an individual who is wrestling with God. He waits patiently for a teachable moment and then speaks a word in season. He is always satisfied, yet always thirsty for more growth in Christ. He does not demand instant answers from God, but he is persuaded that regardless of how things look, God is always faithful and true.

In her article, "How to Comfort the Suffering," Jill Sciacca offers some practical suggestions:

1. Be aggressive in your approach to help. Don't confront one who is suffering and say, "If there is anything I can do, please call me." Rather than relieving responsibility, this creates it. Instead offer specifics. "When can I come and take your children to the zoo?" "Would tomorrow be a good day to come over and clean house for you?" "What do you need from the store?"

2. Use your talents and gifts specifically. Do not put yourself under pressure to perform a task that is undesirable to you. If you do, the chances are great that your attempt to minister may prove meaningless. Instead, carefully consider what you can do and like to do. Then be creative — the possibilities are endless . . .

3. Be sensitive to the real needs of the one suffering. It is a myth, for example, that a hurting person constantly needs company . . . When you do call on the person, resist the temptation to say something profound unless your advice is requested . . . Above all, do not speak beyond your own experience. Telling someone that everything will be all right when you have never known the depths of his or her hardship is an empty statement. Think carefully before sharing scripture, and ask yourself if that which is spoken will communicate comfort or condemnation . . .[2]

But how does someone who feels like "buzzard bait" cope with sincere "buzzards"? Very simply put — *they love them!* When you have been through personal heartache, some people will feel compelled to say something to you about your particular situation. In their awkwardness, they may blurt out irrelevant observations. Others will be drawn to you, thinking you are some kind of "guru." They will pour out their problems to you and may chide you if you have no magical formulas for them. Don't feel pressured by their expectations of you. They are attracted to you because they want to tap into the invisible support system that has enabled you to function during your trials. Whether you like it or not, they probably consider you an expert in knowing how to handle tough times. If you have a word of wisdom for them, share it. If you have nothing specific to communicate to them, admit it with confidence and offer your friendship and prayers.

Personal trauma offers us the opportunity to experience a precious treasure — an understanding heart, a tender heart, a heart filled with mercy.

DISCUSSION GUIDE

1. When you have encountered people who are hurting, do you have a tendency to give pat answers? What are some ways you can express genuine empathy?

2. What are you doing to encourage others?

3. Select three people. Encourage them this week, either by a telephone call, a personal visit or a note.

CHAPTER 11

Mercy
Rewrote a Life

It is a pity that our tears on the account of our troubles should so blind our eyes that we should not see our mercies.

John Flavel

It was Sunday. I had just finished preaching and the service had ended. While talking with various people, I caught sight of a familiar, rather successful businessman in his late twenties (I'll call him Bob). He was standing alone, glancing periodically in my direction. His countenance revealed much about his emotional state. It was the way he stood with shoulders stooped slightly, hands in pockets, leaning against the wall. The way he nervously looked at me with needy, sad eyes — pleading for some kind of help. His dark, disheveled hair and somewhat rumpled casual clothes. The entire scene compelled me to walk over to him. Within seconds, my arm was around Bob's shoulders and without a word we walked to an area where we could talk privately.

For a moment he stood silently, biting his lower lip, looking over my shoulder as if feeling guilty for taking me from my conversation with others.

"Is everything all right?" I queried, breaking the silence.

"No," he responded, shifting his weight from one foot to the other. "I don't know what to do. I'm at wit's end."

In the quietness, I couldn't help but notice how rapidly the tears filled his eyes and then spilled onto his cheeks. *The tears are so close to the surface*, I thought. *He must be experiencing intense pain.* I interrupted my observations with a silent prayer, *Lord, grant me wisdom. Make me a channel of your healing love and care.*

By now Bob's weeping was profuse. He tried to control himself without success.

The last time I had seen him, he was confident, well groomed, and had carried himself in a professional, yet personable manner. What a stark contrast! Standing before me was a vulnerable, despondent man overwhelmed with hopelessness.

I put my arm around his shoulders again. After a few minutes, he heaved a big sigh and began his story.

"Yesterday I discovered that my wife has been having an affair with one of my best friends," he blurted. "I don't know what to do. When I confronted her, she packed her things and moved in with him. It was a big scene. Last night I scared the hell out of myself. I almost blew my brains out with a pistol."

He paused, as if allowing the shock value to penetrate.

"For months I *knew* something was wrong, you know — late nights, stupid excuses, and odd behavior — but I just kept denying it. I kept pushing everything out of my mind. Well, yesterday morning she had left for part of the day and I was cleaning out the attic. In an old suitcase I accidentally found a cache of love notes that must go back six or seven months. I began reading the notes he had written to her and I couldn't believe the stuff he wrote! He was tearing me down left and right. And I thought he was my friend. I can't believe it."

It was a paradox. His eyes were red and swollen. His cheeks were partially moist with some powdery patches of dried tears. Yet at the same time, he began unloading the sordid details found in the notes in an increasingly calm, forced manner.

Finally his speech relaxed and he reflected, "You know, Pastor Freeman, I don't know if this makes any sense to you, but I feel like a total fool. Do you remember the popular song by the Bee Gees about the man who started a joke and got the whole world laughing, but then found out that the joke was on him?"

"Yes," I replied.

"Well, that's me. I'm the one everybody's laughing at. I'm the fool. I feel like the wind has been knocked out of me. I'm going crazy with anger, jealousy and wanting to get revenge. I want to hurt him real bad."

His voice carried a subdued tone. "Please help me. I'm trapped. I don't want to live and yet I don't want to die."

After listening intently, I knew that he would need long-term support to help him through the challenges of denial, wounded pride, retaliation, self righteousness and acceptance. He was like a drowning man, thrashing wildly about, searching for a solution.

I shared some words of encouragement and prayed with him. He gladly accepted my offer to visit together on a weekly basis.

During the initial sessions, Bob poured out his heart, expressing a mixture of hatred, guilt, fear and embarrassment. Many times I looked into his eyes with nothing to offer but my friendship and concern. At these moments, it seemed as though a million questions bombarded my mind. What could I possibly say that would remotely touch his intense encounter with trauma? Why did I feel so awkward and inadequate in his tearful presence? How could I offer advice that didn't sound like a pat answer or a religious cliché? How could I understand the deep pain in his soul and yet challenge him to develop a stable mental attitude?

Over a period of weeks, Bob said he could not sleep many nights and that Psalm 25 was a chapter he would read repeatedly. As I looked at the verses, I could clearly see the pain in his soul. These verses especially seemed to reveal his struggle:

> My eyes are ever on the LORD, for he will release my feet from the snare. Turn unto me and be gracious to me, for I am lonely and afflicted. The troubles of my heart have multiplied, free me from my anguish. Look upon my affliction and my distress and take away all my sins (verses 15-18, NIV).

After a few more sessions, he seemed to slowly accept personal responsibility for actions which contributed to the breakdown of his marriage. Finally, I gave him an assignment between counseling sessions. Bob's homework was to do a thorough study on the subject of mercy and report back.

The following week, he excitedly entered my office with an overwhelming number of conclusions about the prescribed subject. His countenance was different. His voice carried the ring of renewed vitality. Naturally, I was skeptical about the longevity of such dramatic change. But as I listened to the details of his discovery, I could not help but be drawn by the convincing manner in which he presented the information. The following is a condensed version of his findings:

1. Except for the Lord's mercies, every human being in the world would be consumed (even the innocent victim of an affair) (Lamentations 3:22).

2. God concluded that every human was a dirty, rotten sinner, so that He could have mercy upon everybody (Romans 11:32).

3. God is a billionaire when it comes to mercy (Ephesians 2:4).

4. Christians can't even present their bodies as living sacrifices unless they first have received God's mercy (Romans 12:1).

5. Mercy actually jumps up and down for joy because of the great triumph over judgment (James 2:13).

6. Mercy gives a tailor-made provision for every human pressure, enabling people to see the glory of Jesus Christ instead of fainting (2 Corinthians 4:1).

7. All the requirements of truth are satisfied by mercy (Psalm 85:10).

8. The only way Christians can give mercy is if it is first received on a personal basis (Matthew 5:7).

9. Present-day Christians are given the same sure mercies that King David received throughout his lifetime (Acts 13:34).

10. If God could be merciful with the clever manipulator, Jacob, there's hope for others (Genesis 32:10).

11. God's mercy endures forever (Psalms 136:1).

12. Recognition of personal sin is the prerequisite to receiving mercy (Matthew

9:13).
13. Mercy is one of the basic principles that modern-day Pharisees forget (Matthew 23:23).

Bob concluded his enlightening discourse by showing how, in the not-so-distant past, he had been embittered by his wife's extra-marital affair. He had been paralyzed by the "unfairness" of the entire situation. Now he realized that, despite the hurt he felt from his wife's wicked sin of adultery, God had worked the situation for his good. It was the first time in his life that he had been driven to his knees in passionate prayer, to recognize his human goodness as unacceptable in God's sight and plead for His mercy! We wept together in my office, praising God for His mercy.

As with Job, nothing had changed outwardly. Bob's wife was still gone, threatening divorce. His home was still lonely. His wife's side of the bed was still cold at night. His wife's lover was still arrogantly flaunting a repulsive lifestyle. But something had changed — Bob's attitude.

He stopped justifying himself. He quit blaming himself and others. He refrained from gazing at his own navel in self-pity, depression and self-analysis. Instead, he decided to fight back with objective truth from the Word of God. He acknowledged his drastic need for mercy and focused the attention of his heart upon the King of kings and Lord of lords, Jesus Christ. I continued to counsel Bob for a short time after that. I saw him grow by leaps and bounds.

Much later, I took advantage of an opportunity to see how Bob was progressing. It saddened me to hear of his wife's ultimate decision to reject his attempts at reconciliation and divorce him. However, I was heartened by his settled conviction about the matter. In spite of all the hurtful events that had transpired up to that moment, he was joyful about the new-found maturity he was experiencing.

I have concluded that the secret of Bob's physical, mental, emotional, and spiritual health was his decision to continue in the spirit of mercy. When he awakened every morning, he thanked God for the mercy which allowed him to be alive for another day. When he ate his breakfast, he acknowledged that because of God's mercy he could chew and digest his food.

His ability to function well on the job was appreciated because of mercy. He was grateful for every small detail in

life. The disciplined attitude of gratitude caused him to steer
away from the debilitating effects of self-pity and propelled
him into an exciting adventure, giving mercy as freely as it
was received. Mercy was like a telescope that brought the
heavenly perspective into sharp focus.

Truly, it was God's abundant mercy that rewrote Bob's life.

DISCUSSION GUIDE

1. Is God rewriting your life as He did for Bob?

2. How have God's mercies affected you during this past
year?

3. Someone has said that God's mercy withholds what
we deserve and His grace gives us what we do not deserve.
Think about that which you rightfully deserve in the eyes of
a holy God and that which you do not deserve, but which
God in His love bestows upon you. Rejoice today in His mercy
and grace.

CHAPTER 12

Wow, It's Real!

*Look upon your chastenings as God's chariots
sent to carry your soul into the high places of
spiritual achievement.*

Hannah Whitall Smith

Q. What is fifteen hundred miles square,
   is enclosed by a sheer wall
   two hundred and sixteen feet thick,
   with twelve gates made of pearls
   (from rather large oysters, I presume),
   and twelve foundations made of precious stones
   like beryl and amethyst,
   has streets constructed of pure,
   transparent gold (no prospecting allowed),
   has custom-built mansions of indescribable beauty,
   has no ambulance sirens, no pain, no tears, no death,
   no darkness; has a crystal clear river
   with fruitful trees on either bank,
   has an innumerable company of angels flying about,
   has a sea of glass (with fish in it, I hope),
   has people from earth who have graduated to it,
   and above all, has the throne of God with a

green rainbow overhead?
A. The heavenly city.

Can you sense the excitement? This is an attempt to
describe the place that is promised to those who have made
the choice to follow Jesus. This is the location where crowns
and rewards will be given to those who have received Jesus
as personal Savior and who have faithfully performed the
details of the kingdom of God with dignity. This is the city
where all secrets will be revealed and where all wrongs will
be righted. This is the place where all "why?" questions will
be answered. This is our destiny!

Upon our arrival in that beautiful city we'll fall to our
faces at the feet of Jesus. We'll look up, seeing Him in all His
glory and splendor — face to face with the One who knows
everything about us and still loves us. Then we'll see the
nailprints in His hands and feet and the mark of the spearpoint
in His side (the only things in heaven that are made by
humans). We'll be overwhelmed by His personal attention.

As eternity unfolds, we will also want to interview all
the saints of old. We will ask Elijah to tell the inside story
about his dramatic departure from earth to heaven in a fiery
chariot. We will ask Methuselah how many push-ups he could
do at 968 years of age. We will want to participate in Peter's
excitement as he relates his secret for successful water walking.
Then, we will ask to hear Rahab's story of how her house
stood while the walls of Jericho collapsed. As each one shares
his or her personal adventure, something will be unique about
each one. None of them will be griping about the "unfairness"
of God.

In reality, Job won't be grumbling about his earthly trials.
Moses won't be grouching about his wilderness journey. John
the Baptist won't be complaining about the loss of his head.
David won't be grumping about his troubles with Saul. Each
one will magnify the perfect justice and mercy of God. They
will refer to every human event from an eternal perspective.

Won't it be refreshing? Just imagine: Every communication
will honor Jesus. Every human drama will be related in absolute
truth from God's point of view. Every person's motives will
be unhindered by pride, selfishness or sentimentality.

After speaking with a host of saints and angels, we will
probably want to make our way to a little-known mansion.
Before continuing, allow me to put my tongue in my cheek.

Equipped with thousands of video consoles, it is called "Comedy Palace." This palace is there for the personal enjoyment of each Christian.

We will be able to push a button and instantly recall selected earthly moments when we were depressed, anxious or angry. From our heavenly vantage point we will be able to see the real reasons behind our reactions. We'll chuckle reverently as we replay those instances when circumstances seemed dark and gloomy and it felt like God was on vacation. We'll giggle when we see how brattily we behaved when we thought God was treating us "unfairly," that maybe we were the brunt of some celestial practical joke.

We will be able to laugh at human responses to life's situations because we will possess the perfect ability to know as God knows. We'll see how valuable it would have been to live with a constant hope, undiminished by problems. While basking in heaven's glory, we will see that all our emotional and physical turmoil was nothing when compared to the splendor of eternity.

As I put my tongue back in place, let's meditate on the reality of that beautiful city. When things get tough here on earth, let's allow His perspective to become ours. When tragedy strikes, we can permit the tears to flow while yielding to the sweetness of His presence. When the intensity of the battle becomes much more than we originally bargained for, let's not become grim; instead, let's enjoy a practical sense of humor and keep on keeping on, never losing our fervent hunger for His Word.

When all is said and done, God owns everything. He owns our children, our bodies, our finances, and our spouses. He holds our past, present and future in the palm of His hand. We are stewards, but not owners. He gives. He takes away. Blessed be the Name of our Lord. Naked we enter into this world and naked we go from it.

What helps us experience heaven while on earth? What assists us in keeping eternal value in clear view? What keeps us joyfully advancing when every bone and tissue in our body is yelling, "Quit! Throw in the towel"? What shows us the clear lines separating stewardship and ownership? What reveals the immortal justice of God?

The cross of Jesus Christ . . .

DISCUSSION GUIDE

1. If you were provided the opportunity to visit "Comedy Palace" tomorrow afternoon, what would be three selected "unfair" events you would observe on the video console? How do you think you'd react?

2. In view of Nehemiah 8:10, in what ways does the joy of the Lord strengthen you?

3. Name three things about heaven that make your present suffering worthwhile.

CHAPTER 13

Scandalized

*The bitterest cup with Christ is better than the
sweetest cup without Him.*

Ian MacPherson

Pause and think, just for a moment, about the spotless
Lamb, Jesus Christ. On the cross, He accomplished what no
self-help program could do. With excruciating pain, He took
upon His precious body the sins of the entire world — past,
present, and future. He became our sin, reeking with the
wicked, vile stench of homosexuality, adultery, thievery, pride,
bitterness, lying and rebellion. He identified with us to such
a degree that His Father could not look upon Him as He paid
the penalty for our sins.

He glared at death, as if to say, "Where is your sting?
Where is your holding power?"

He stared at every foul demon in hell, as if to say, "Where
is your plan? Where is your strength?"

He scrutinized Satan as if to say, "Where is your fulfill-
ment? Where is your satisfaction?"

He gazed at every human being who ever lived as if to
say, "I love you this much. Will you receive My death as the

payment for your sins?"

And then He looked at His Father and said, "Into Your hands I commend My spirit."

He finished His work. He accomplished His mission. He died.

With the cross in clear view, permit me to ask some probing questions:

What is your primary support system in life? Is it your health? Your job? Your family? Your wealth?

To what do you turn in the midst of a crisis? Do you panic? Do you eat a lot? Do you sleep a lot? Do you work a lot?

How do you react when treated "unfairly"? Do you want revenge? Do you rant and rave behind closed doors? Do you harbor bitterness? Do you ache quietly?

While these questions are difficult to answer, at times we become sickened by the conditions of our hearts. At every funeral we become painfully aware of our mortality. We clearly see how fragile we are. We see how quickly tragedy can strike. (At one moment they were in the car, laughing and joking. A split second later, they were dead.) It's easy to become cynical. It's easy to develop an existential posture — life without meaning.

In our search for answers, we turn to the Bible, hoping to find meaning in the midst of a suffering world. Our brows become furrowed as we come across some of the following hard sayings from the lips of Jesus, wondering why He seems to be making life more complicated than it already is:

> Do not suppose that I have come to bring peace to the earth. I did not come to bring peace, but a sword. For I have come to turn a man against his father, a daughter against her mother, a daughter-in-law against her mother-in-law (Matthew 10:34,35, NIV).

> Follow me, and let the dead bury their own dead (Matthew 8:22, NIV).

> If anyone would come after me, he must deny himself and take up his cross and follow Me (Matthew 16:24, NIV).

> Jesus . . . said, "Go, sell everything you have and give to the poor, and you will have treasure in heaven. Then come, and follow Me." At this the man's face fell (Mark 10:21,22, NIV).

Unless a kernel of wheat falls to the ground and dies, it remains only a single seed (John 12:24, NIV).

As we read these harsh statements from Jesus, we may struggle with various rationalizations: We may want to believe that He meant something entirely different for the people who were actually in His presence. Maybe Jesus didn't really mean to make such stringent demands upon weak, frail human beings. Or possibly, He was merely reacting to the unique social pressures from that particular time in human history that are unrelated to the challenges of contemporary Christianity.

Whatever our automatic responses may be, the truth of the matter is that Jesus' all-or-nothing message is just as vital today as it was when He walked the earth. He came to die so that we might live.

Some 2,000 years ago, Jesus was confronted by hearts that were spiritually cold and indifferent. It doesn't take very long for the careful student of the Scriptures to realize that gentle Jesus went out of His way to offend various people. At one point, the disciples cautioned Jesus by telling Him that the Pharisees were offended by His actions and words (Matthew 15:12). On another occasion, the Pharisees were motivated by hard-core bitterness as they tried to belittle Him with the scathing words, "Is not this the carpenter, the son of Mary?" (Mark 6:3).

Jesus healed on the Sabbath and allowed His disciples to pluck corn on the Sabbath. All of this was calculated to produce a response that revealed the true hearts of casual observers. Even His disciples were offended by Him on a number of occasions (Mark 14:27-29).

In order for us to understand this properly, we must find the meaning of the word "offend" in the Greek language. The original rendering is *skandalizō*[1] from which we get the English term "to scandalize." The word literally means to shock a person by outrageous means, which in turn arouses human prejudice.

In the New Testament, Jesus discerned many "sacred cows" among the people of His day. He then went about diligently smashing each "sacred cow." Of course, this action was not enthusiastically received. Hatred for Him grew with each passing day. At the appointed time, He set His face toward Jerusalem to die.

Why did the multitudes turn against this One who cared
enough to speak the truth? The answer is simple. He refused
to co-exist with sentimental relationships. He brought the
authenticity of the cross into every transaction.

It is interesting to note that upon His death His disciples
were deeply offended, or shall we say, scandalized by Him.
His crucifixion caused fear, anger, and disillusionment to penetrate the heart of each disciple. Without the cross, they
probably would have gone through life struggling with super-
ficiality and periodic backsliding.

But, thanks be to God, they were confronted with and
outraged by the fact that Jesus the Messiah, their Messiah,
was crucified in weakness! Before Calvary, they had a passive
understanding of who Jesus really was, but after the Resurrection and Pentecost, their convictions about Jesus caused them
to be fearless soldiers of the cross. Every disciple was tortured
and flogged. Eleven of the disciples finally faced a cruel martyr's
death without wavering:

1. Peter — crucified with head downwards
2. James, son of Zebedee — the sword
3. John — natural death (after surviving a
   cauldron of boiling oil)
4. Andrew — crucified slowly (bound by
   cords)
5. James, son of Alphaeus — crucified
6. Thomas — spear thrust
7. Simon — crucified
8. Bartholomew — crucified
9. Thaddaeus — killed by arrows
10. Matthew — the sword
11. James, brother of Jesus — stoned
12. Philip — crucified

Something great had happened! The disciples were
changed. Calvary's weakness had to precede their infilling of
power and direction by the Holy Spirit at Pentecost.

The great Christian writer A. W. Tozer once commented
that God cannot use a person until he or she has been hurt
deeply (and, therefore, those of us who have been hurt deeply
can take comfort). As in Bible times, pain seems to be one of
the only messages we can clearly understand. God uses it to

get our attention.

Emotional pain caused by "unfair" circumstances is hard to bear. When we get hurt, we become irrational and unreasonable. God uses physical and emotional suffering, however, to create an environment whereby we ultimately are forced to confront our inability to continue in human strength.

Usually God uses people as instruments in this process, so we also struggle with hatred and revenge. We focus on people (rather than God's plan), which scandalizes us and arouses our prejudices. By focusing on the "fairness" of our circumstances, we lose the whole purpose of the God-ordained trial and slowly grind ourselves into the ground with a root of bitterness.

God uses people, places and things to cause us to face the wickedness of our hearts. It is then that we fall down at the front of the cross to humbly receive His tailor-made provision of forgiveness and mercy for our specific need. He takes our acknowledged sin, casts it in the deepest sea, and then fills us with resurrection power to meet the next challenge.

It is rare, in the 20th century, to find people who have gone through devastating circumstances and have entered into the realm of spiritual maturity with "treasures hidden in darkness and riches stored in secret places" (Isaiah 45:3). It is unusual to find those who have crashed through the maturity barriers of moods, mental blocks and prejudices that have challenged them in the midst of personal trauma.

The popularization of an incomplete gospel message has inoculated the masses with a mere caricature of Jesus, causing many to know Him as Savior, but not as Lord. The offense of the cross is considered vulgar, while the modern gospel of convenience is popularized.

In the thick of severe testings, it is easy to withdraw our absolute trust in His sovereignty. That is why we must not only comprehend the meaning of the cross, but we must also take up our cross (our place of death — our electric chair, if you will) daily and apply the principles of death, burial and resurrection in every detail of our lives.

With abundant clarity we see that there are no caste systems, no race distinctions, no human opinions, and no all-consuming "fairness" questions. At the foot of the cross we learn to operate in faith without emotional support. We realize that we are not our own; we have been purchased by a great price — the precious blood of Jesus (1 Corinthians 6:20).

This allows us to conclude that God uses people, places, and things as tools to bring us to our wits' ends. Money will not be needed in heaven. But on earth, it is a tool used to teach us the adventures of stewardship. Marriage as we currently know it will not be realized in heaven. But on earth it is a sacred means by which God can teach us the art of forgiveness and unconditional love. Diseased and paralyzed bodies will not be present in eternity. But in this world, they can provide great opportunities for people to experience patience, quietness, and confidence. Unjust criticism will not be heard in paradise. But here on this planet we learn to face it with honesty, mercy, and a sense of humor.

Instead of allowing human events to stop us, we progress in a perpetual forward motion, permitting the death of the cross to scandalize us by striking at the root of personal selfishness. In turn, we step outside of our puny worlds and minister the resurrection love of Jesus Christ to those who are imprisoned by self-pity because of "unfair" circumstances.

Earl was this type of guy. I heard him preach to a bunch of inmates in the state penitentiary. What a powerful message he gave as he told his life's story!

Right from the start, his life was doomed. "I was born in the ghetto of New York City. My momma was a whore. I never knew my daddy. From early on, I learned to steal for survival. By the age of nine, I had joined a gang, was hooked on drugs and had taken part in five murders. The law was constantly on my tail."

As I listened to this short, compact man of swarthy complexion, I was deeply touched by his intensity. He went on to relate a horror story filled with true but almost unbelievable events. I wondered how anyone could survive.

Yet, his voice became tender as he shared how Christ had changed his life and had given him a new purpose for living. It was as if his words were transporting everyone's imagination out of that cold, sterile meeting room and into the presence of the living God. There was hardly a dry eye in the place. Even the guards were visibly moved by the drama.

Earl had every legitimate reason under the sun to give up and be a failure. But instead he allowed the cross to work the love of Christ into his life. Out of this came a potent ministry of genuine hope to many who were hurting.

In summary, there is no way to avoid emotional wounds. They are a realistic part of being alive. We can, however, understand that God authorizes the permission necessary for wounding experiences to offend us, so that we will be challenged to leave our comfort zones and enter into a new level of maturity in our Christian walk.

If we play the blame game, we merely prolong what must happen anyway. God will continue to probe the conditions of our hearts with various and sundry circumstances until we confront our disguised pride and receive His mercy. When we respond to His provision of grace we receive the capacity to pass through, not park in, even deeper valleys filled with the shadows of death — fearing no evil.

DISCUSSION GUIDE

1. Emotional pain seems to be an integral part of God's plan in bringing us to the place of spiritual maturity. Why do you think there is no shortcut to maturity?

2. What does the cross mean to you?

3. How has God "scandalized" you? How have you reacted?

CHAPTER 14

Sirens
and Smoke

*It is wonderful what God can do with the broken
heart, if He gets all the pieces.*

George Mueller

That blasted phone! In the darkened bedroom I could
clearly see the glaring red numbers on the digital clock: *12:43.*
Moments before, I had been jolted by the cruel sound of the
ringing telephone. In a semi-comatose state I climbed out of
my warm bed, struggled with my bathrobe, and then stumbled
to the phone. I had no idea how long it had been ringing.

It had been a full day. My pastoral responsibilities had
included Saturday-morning visitations, hosting a regular radio
talk show, studying for Sunday's sermon and dinner with
family and friends. I had been asleep for at least an hour.

"Yes?" I managed groggily after fumbling with the receiver.

"Is this Reverend Freeman?" she inquired in an official
sounding tone.

Upon my affirmative reply, she acquainted me with her
name and her status as a nurse at the emergency room of a
local hospital. "Reverend Freeman," she continued, "I have been
instructed to inform you that a family from your church has

experienced a fire in their home within the past hour. Are you familiar with the Henrys?"

"Yes," I responded. My thoughts began to race. I could barely concentrate on her next words.

"At this present time, John and Shirley [the parents] are being retained here for a while for smoke inhalation treatment. Larry [the seven-year-old] is in critical condition with 95 percent of his body burned. Josh [eleven years old] was burned, but his condition is not known. Both boys are in the ambulance on their way to the Burn Center at Baltimore City Hospital. John and Shirley have requested that you go directly to Baltimore City Hospital."

I was dumbfounded. What could I say?

"Any questions?" she added.

"N-No. Thank you," I stammered. "Tell them I'll leave immediately. Thank you. Goodbye."

I put the receiver back into place and felt myself hunching over, with both hands on the kitchen counter — staring blankly at the pattern imprinted in the formica. I let out a long sigh as the impact of what I had just heard slowly settled into my mind.

Numbly, I walked back to the bedroom. My wife was wide awake. As I dressed, I explained the situation to her as I had heard it. Moments later I walked outside into the brisk, wintry blast of air. The forty-minute drive seemed like an eternity with a hundred questions bombarding my mind. Was Larry going to make it? How did the fire start? How badly was Josh burned? Were John and Shirley all right? Was the house completely destroyed? Why did this have to happen to such a fine family? What could I possibly say that would minister to the parents and relatives? Why was I feeling so inadequate?

When I arrived, one of Shirley's brothers and his wife were already present in the waiting room. They gave me a sketchy account of the grim situation. Over the next hour, the room began to fill with relatives and close family friends. The burn unit was a beehive of activity as Larry and Josh were given expert attention.

A while later, the pathetic-looking figures of John and Shirley stepped off the elevator. Glazed eyes filled with a mixture of fear and pain. Smudged faces and hands. Winter coats hastily thrown over long johns and pajamas. Not much could be said, so I held them. They wept quietly.

We all found our separate seats and waited for the
progress reports on Josh and Larry. Approximately an hour
went by with waves of tears followed by pensive silence.
Around 4:30 A.M., the doctor's presence caused everyone to
bristle to attention, searching for clues on his worn face. He
broke the news gently but firmly. Larry had died. John and
Shirley desperately clutched each other. They sobbed uncontroll-
ably.

Josh's condition progressed rapidly with intermittent moments of uncertainty. The days leading up to and following
Larry's funeral were challenging for everyone concerned — especially John and Shirley.

Listen between the lines as Shirley recounts those events
that happened nine months ago. I did not dare to retouch the
words, afraid that I might spoil their essence. With great
respect, I thank her for putting her feelings on paper and then
granting permission to share them.

> After the fire was under control, fire engines were
> everywhere. The noise, the stench of fire and water
> caused an overwhelming urge to vomit. (My memory up
> to this point is vivid, but I'm just not able to put it on
> paper.)
>
> Our boys were each in a different ambulance. My
> husband and I were in a third. Fear. This was the most
> fearful time in my life. The sound of sirens shook me
> to the core. This time the sirens were for us. It was my
> house. My home. My children. I didn't just read it in
> the paper or know the people somehow. It was me.
>
> In the ambulance, surprisingly, my husband and I were
> able to talk. Guarding each word, considering the emo-
> tional state of the other. We prayed constantly on this
> fifteen-minute ride to the hospital. Our prayer and conver-
> sation mingled in a very unique way as we were intensely
> aware of God's presence. It wasn't necessary to say, "Let's
> pray." From this time on, my husband and I were united
> in a brand-new way. At the cross.
>
> A few days later, sitting across the room from a
> smaller-than-usual, closed casket, I was gripped with the
> realization that Larry was a smaller-than-usual person.
> He just hadn't grown enough to die. Larry was just seven.
> He was (to me, anyway) everything a seven-year-old
> should be. Cute, happy, ever so kind, not too bright in
> school, so wonderful to hug and he loved me. He was

just a baby. My baby. Larry was supposed to grow up
and I was supposed to die first. I was numb, but not
too numb.

God sat so close to me on that bench. He had never
before been closer. Heaven was so close and *real*. An
attitude of worship totally encompassed me. I was being
comforted by Almighty God.

As I write this, I am weeping. The pain is just as
great as ever. The weeks and months spent mourning
leave me faint.

Always running to Him like a baby. Daily. Moment by
moment. And every single time He's there! Waiting to
wipe away my tears as a mother would her son.

When my life fell apart before my eyes, I accused God
of not knowing my pain because He was never a mother.
I was wrong. Through it all, I learned to call Him "Abba,
Father. Daddy."

Suddenly the entire past is equal. Infancy, toddlerhood,
kindergarten and second grade are all the same. The
progression of life has stopped. They all *were*, nothing
is. There is no present. There will be no tomorrow.

A very few weeks ago I was at the grocery store.
Outside, there were boys eagerly waiting to carry grocery
bags. They were so full of life. My heart became physically
heavy and I began to sob.

Yelling once again to God, "Larry was going to do that.
He was going to be kind to people and even handsome.
It is not fair. He was going to be a fine, young Christian
man. Close to you. He was already studying your Word
in school and at home with us."

Well, I've never heard God speak in an audible voice,
but His response was perfectly clear — what peace swept
over me! I was able to rejoice. God once again had to
remind me that He was in control all the time. God's
plan was not my plan. God's thoughts were different
from my thoughts.

Perhaps that is when I realized that Larry was never
truly mine. I was just a steward.

As I look at my new little baby, Jacob, in the infant
seat next to me, I see him so fragile, just three months
old. I say to him, "You're not mine, either."

Face to face with the sovereignty of God!

Each time I read this account, my eyes well up with
tears, knowing that God has specifically comforted each one
in this human drama. Some people get bitter when faced with
similar trauma. But John and Shirley have allowed this trial

to tenderize their hearts and make them even sweeter. Life
has not been easy for them. At times certain memories will
strike without warning and they will weep and then stop as
quickly as they began. Both of them have endured dry seasons
with spent emotions and emptiness.

Through it all, they have permitted the cross of Jesus
Christ to work out their natural resources and then work in
the fruit of the Holy Spirit. Even though they have not consis-
tently felt warm, fuzzy feelings, they have mutually decided
to experience God's joy regardless of the circumstances. They
have adjusted to God's justice, seeing the loss of their home
and the death of their son as an opportunity to view an
inexplicable event from His perspective. They have been re-
warded with superabundant grace from the hand of God.

It reminds me of the apostle Paul's statement in Philippians 3:10. He said that he had mentally counted everything
in his life to be loss. But when he actually suffered the loss
of all things, he entered into an advanced phase of maturity
that was forced by a series of "unfair" experiences. These
terrifying events provided fertilizer with which he could mix
the soil of his heart and grow into a new level of fellowship
with Jesus Christ in the power of His resurrection so that he,
Paul, could rejoice in the midst of even greater suffering.

DISCUSSION GUIDE

1. Through which trials do you think God has sought
to increase your patience?

2. Do you agree that a crisis is necessary to apply faith?
Why or why not?

3. Do you have the attitude that all you have is owned
by God and is merely entrusted to you as a steward? How
do you know?

CHAPTER 15

Innocence Lost, Purity Gained

*Affliction to the people of God is the pruning
knife to the vine to prepare for greater fruitfulness.*
                                                    Anonymous

There is a difference between innocence and purity.
I happened upon this truth some time ago as a woman was
relating to me the grim details of her bout with cancer. She
painted a verbal picture of her rosy, almost fairy-tale life before
doctors discovered that her body was loaded with disease.
That discovery smashed her rose-colored glasses. As she graphically described the struggle that ensued, she observed that,
somewhere in the middle of her emotional battle, she lost her
innocence.

As I listened to her real-life drama, I couldn't help but
be struck by her statement. I began to think.

Babies are innocent. Babies have never experienced severe
testing. As children mature, they go through the turbulent
years of adolescence. Ideally, they complete all the necessary
developmental tasks and enter into the scary world of adult-
hood.

Somewhere along the line, however, they get rocked by

a gut-wrenching, agonizing, weeping-until-there-are-no-more-tears-left trial. It is inevitable. It happens to every human being. Change the faces and the places — it occurs in the life of every person. It is necessary. It destroys the illusion that everything is OK, then it explodes the belief system that tells us that what we have belongs to us. It tears down the cognitive distortion involved in the belief that the pleasures of this world satisfy and are enough for us.

It may come and then disappear months later, leaving us with a new frame of reference, or it may stay with us till we die, as a constant reminder of our need to depend on Him as we should. It may draw the agnostic to Jesus. On the flip side, it may cause the Christian to rely upon Jesus in a brand-new way. Whatever it is, it causes us to lose our innocence. It forces change.

We are compelled to re-evaluate our purpose in life and are motivated to make a series of important decisions. We may end up choosing the cynical route, buttressed by a predictable pattern of intellectual arguments, or we may submit under the mighty hand of God, saying, "It is not my will that is important. May Your will be done in and through me. I love You. I am not living for my benefit but for Your honor and glory. Whatever You sovereignly choose for my life is OK with me. But please give me the grace and strength to handle the pain. Along with Job I say, 'Though You slay me, yet will I trust You.'"

Granted, this is in the category of dangerous prayers. You know, prayers like: "Lord, make me humble." or "Lord, please teach me patience." Watch out! (I have long since stopped praying like that. I figure that He is going to implement the answer to those prayers in His own time, whether I like it or not.) I think, however, that God desires to develop within our souls a simple attitude of humility and availability.

Take Chip for instance. He asked the Lord to work humility into his life. As a pastor of a thriving congregation in the South, he was enraged by the means chosen to plow the soil of his heart. He lost his innocence during a massive split in his church. The pettiness, gossip and juvenile behavior exhibited during the in-fighting cause him to harbor bitterness in his heart toward God and Christianity.

The group in the church that was more powerful turned against Chip and triumphantly ousted him from his pastoral position. He secured a job in auto sales and was so disillusioned that he refused to darken the door of any church for more than a year. My heart wept for him during our many late-night phone conversations as he bitterly recounted the unscriptural, unethical tactics that were used against him.

Did he come through? Yes. Actually, the Lord used the "unfair" chain of events to convict him of some deeply rooted Pharisaical tendencies. He became stronger than ever before. In fact, as I write these words, Chip and his family are fruitful missionaries in Europe.

What do we gain when innocence is lost? Must we become embittered, developing a thick exterior? I think not. Heat changes gold and silver into a liquid state so that the dross can be cleared away. In the same way, intense pain softens up the heart, dislodging the temporal values that contaminate, permitting the Holy Spirit and the Word of God the opportunity to purify the motives of the individual involved.

God makes us pure by His grace but uses trials to test our capacity for implementing that grace. The believer who has been tried by unexpected difficulties and has passed each test with "God's Good Housekeeping Seal of Approval" upon his or her life, will enter into the category of purity.

"Blessed are the pure in heart; for they shall see God" (Matthew 5:8). Having a crisp, clearly focused vision of eternal value depends upon the integrity of our character during the test of sudden trials. If we rail against God's supposed lack of "fairness," we miss the whole point and merely prolong the inevitable.

Jesus has satisfied the requirements of justice through His death. He now provides us with an eternal support system that allows us to reject fearlessly all natural wisdom and trust Him with reckless abandon. He is on our side. His is not playing mind games with us. He is determined to make our souls prosper. Our daily challenge is to *continue* in the Word that has already made us free (John 8:31-32).

DISCUSSION GUIDE

1. Name a challenge you are facing today. Plan to face it head on rather than run from it.

2. Have you lost your innocence? If so, have you become bitter or better? In what ways?

3. Do you see God's love and care for you in the circumstances He has planned and allowed? In what ways?

CHAPTER **16**

Skyscraper Theology

*Sorrow is a fruit: God does not make it grow
on limbs too weak to bear it.*

Victor Hugo

"See the man over there looking at the blueprint?
Go ask him. He'll tell you everything you want to know." Following the pointed finger of the sweaty construction worker,
I picked my way carefully through the rocks and dirt. The
man with the blueprint looked up with an inquisitive expression. "Son, may I help you?" he asked.

"Oh, yes, sir," I answered. "I don't want to take much
of your time, but my curiosity has gotten the best of me. I
was hoping you could explain something for my benefit. You
see, over the past few months I have passed this site a number
of times. I've always seen hard-working men all over the place.
But nothing seems to be happening. There's no building yet,
just a big, gaping hole in the ground and—"

Boy, did he ever take me to school! Before I had a chance
to finish, he began to explain some of the intricate details
involved in the design and construction of a high-rise building.

I must have "uh-huhed" and said, "Oh, I see" about 300

times. He told me how the height of the building determined the width and depth of the concrete footings that went into the ground and also the size and number of the steel reinforcing bars that were placed in the ground before the pouring of the cement.

He showed me the blueprints and related that it had already taken more than two years of planning, drawing, meetings with the zoning board and the expenditure of thousands of dollars to bring the crew to their current phase of construction. He also stated that the plans for a building this tall forced them to dig down to rock and then pour tons of concrete upon the rock to establish a suitable foundation.

After thanking him for his kindness in educating a willing learner, I returned to my vehicle and drove away with a brand-new respect for those involved in the many stages of the construction industry.

The project I had just visited entailed much advanced planning; site approval; demolition of previous lot coverage; excavation and the dumping of truckloads of cement; and the strategic placement of steel reinforcement bars. All of this work — and still there were no visible, above-ground results!

Many moons have passed since that episode, yet to this day I cannot get away from an analogy that came to me. What I witnessed and heard at that dusty, noisy construction site is an amazingly accurate story of what happens in all our lives.

So much of the work God does and allows in our lives is unglamorous, employing vast amounts of time with little or no measurable progress. We also find it extremely difficult to understand the reasons why life seems to be treating us so "unfairly."

Stop for a moment and try to imagine yourself as a building. How tall is the building? Is it a one-story structure? A ten-story edifice? Or maybe a forty- or fifty-story skyscraper?

You see, the height determines how deeply God must dig before laying the proper foundation. No humans can handle the elevation of God's blessing without the corresponding work of the cross cutting to the core of the soul. God promotes prepared people.

Ask Joseph. He was a skyscraper. As a youngster, he had a dream that, when it was revealed, made him the object of intense hatred and violence from his older brothers. You can imagine him huddling in the bottom of an empty pit in the

wilderness or stumbling along as a purchased slave in the dust
of an Ishmaelite camel on its way to Egypt. All the while
wondering if maybe he had improperly interpreted the dream
about the twelve sheaves in the field, the sun, the moon, and
the eleven stars. Maybe it didn't mean that his family would
bow down before him and make obeisance to him after all.

To make matters worse, upon arrival in Egypt he was
framed by his new master's wife. When Joseph refused to be
sexually seduced by her, it looked like he was preparing for
a career in prison (Genesis 37-50). Things looked grim and
they also looked "unfair." But God was only excavating the
dirt for a firm foundation for this skyscraper.

Before all was said and done, Joseph became governor
over all the land of Egypt and was used mightily by God to
help thousands of people during a severe famine. Years passed
and his dream was fulfilled. Joseph could then proclaim to his
brothers, "You plotted evil against me, but God turned it into
good, in order to preserve the lives of many people who are
alive today because of what happened" (See Genesis 50:20).
God promotes people who will allow Him to prepare the soil
of their hearts for solid foundations.

But how does God prepare us? My friend, it is in the
school of suffering. I wish there were some other easier answer.
Afflictions that come in the form of uncontrollable events or
nasty, critical people are some of the trials God uses to dig
away the dirt and get down to the bedrock. During these
times, it hurts deeply. The pain is unbearable.

In the meantime, Satan isn't sleeping. He portrays pain
as illogical, unreasonable and "unfair." He desires for us to
remain as one-story people with tiny, one-story capacities for
the foundational riches discovered in God's Word, the Bible.
Satan also tries to cause us to harbor mental-attitude sins of
jealousy and envy toward Christians who are growing in their
walk with the Lord.

While God is using circumstances to dig and blast in
preparation for the foundation, there seems to be no spiritual
progress. No visible results appear above the surface. In fact,
our mental, emotional and spiritual lives actually seem to be
in confusion and upheaval. It is during these times, however,
that we need to take heart, to encourage ourselves in the Lord
and refuse to faint. We must fortify ourselves with the lively
hope that benefits us with maturity in time and rewards in
eternity.

The choice is up to you. God will not violate your freedom of choice. Do you want to be a normal, one-story person with a shallow foundation and convenient, comfortable, predictable Christianity that gets tossed to and fro with every storm? Or do you want to be a skyscraper person who bleeds every situation for every bit of maturity you can squeeze from it? How about it? Just dutifully existing in life, or attacking it with unbridled enthusiasm?

You may be saying, "But my foundation has already been laid and the building program in my life is in its advanced stages. Recently, the Zoning Board of heaven ruled that any further construction would present serious potential damage to myself, my family and my neighbors. They based their ruling on the sub-standard material I chose and the shortcuts I employed with planning and building my life. In other words, my life doesn't meet the universal regulations of God's building code. What am I to do?"

You have two options:

1. Ignore the warning. Keep on building. Attain new, precarious heights of success and prosperity. Eat, drink and be merry. Enjoy life for the present flush of excitement and entertainment. Run with the in-crowd. Avoid spiritual principles at all cost. They might make you uncomfortable and make you think about the consequences of your avoidance mentality and behavior.

2. Heed the warning. Stop construction. Separate who you are from the plans you used. Walk in humility before God while He uses the Word, His precious Holy Spirit, and possibly some "unfair" circumstances to assist in demolishing the old so He can establish the new. God will use His blueprints, His building material, and His construction techniques. It will be worth the honesty and the pain.

DISCUSSION GUIDE

1. In what ways do you identify with Joseph?

2. Think back on a time when you had no visible results of maturity evident in your life. How did you trust God during that time of self-doubt?

3. God promotes prepared people. Meditate on this truth and apply it to your life today.

CHAPTER 17

God Can, But Sometimes Won't

*A full and complete reading of the New Testament
will show conclusively that God has not promised
to solve our problems or answer our questions or
melt away our tribulations. If we can ever get our
sense of values in proper Christian focus, we will
come to understand that the loving presence of God
in the trial furnace is a far greater blessing than
the elimination of trouble by divine intervention.*
Erwin G. Tieman

*O*mnipotence. Aren't you impressed with the way I started off the final chapter of the book with such a fancy-shmancy word? If you're not, I still won't let you spoil it for me — I'm impressed!

Question: What does this noble, awe-inspiring word mean? Answer: God is all-powerful. Period. He can do anything. He can heal all diseases and empty all hospital wards. He can eradicate all crime and stop the abuse of all innocent victims. He can extinguish all wars and squash out all injustice. He can bring harmony to all people and feed all hungry stomachs. He can alleviate all problems that cause mortal agony and eliminate physical death. Get the picture? He can do everything. No, ifs, ands, or buts. He has all power.

We must understand that God's omnipotence is never in question when it comes to freedom from suffering. There is no crisis from which there is no deliverance, since deliverance can come through life or through physical death. Rather, liberation from pain and trauma is a question of His *sovereignty.*

Question: OK now, what does this magnificent word, *sovereignty,* mean? Answer: God will do anything He wants to do, bound only by His own character. In other words, if freedom from a situation that produces pain is a part of His master plan, the individual will be rescued; if not, God has another purpose for the life of the person that is guaranteed to bring Him the most glory. Period.

If He wants to deliver Daniel from the salivating jaws of hungry lions, or let James get decapitated, or let Peter experience an angelic escort from prison, or permit thousands of Christians to get martyred in Roman colosseums, or to allow His only Son, Jesus, to suffer the cruel death of crucifixion to satisfy His justice, He will.

Brian understands this principle. He has learned it the hard way. His eighteen-year-old eyes communicate mischief as he tries to run over my toes with his souped-up electric wheelchair. (Remind me to wear my steel-toed boots next time I visit him.)

Four years ago Brian was riding his ten-speed bicycle when a drunken driver careened across the median strip and hit him broadside. Brian pitched head over heals for thirty yards. The next thing he remembered was the soft touch of a nurse's hand on his forehead — five days later.

As a paraplegic, Brian has battled the icy grip of self-pity. He's grappled with the seductive whisper of suicide. But you know what? He has won a tremendous victory — he has accepted God's sovereignty in the whole matter.

Brian's physical condition has made marginal improvements. His attitude, however, has made a 180-degree turn, from cyclical bouts with rage and hopelessness to sparkling eyes filled with an eternal purpose for living. He has become a "wounded healer," comforting others wherein he has been comforted.

I have joined many others in praying for Brian's healing. Remember, God's omnipotence reveals that He can instantly heal even a young man required by the facts of medical science to spend the rest of his days in a wheel chair. But God's omnipotence is not in question. The real issue is His sovereignty.

Will God get more glory out of a miraculous healing that baffles the doctors with their X-rays and empirical data? Or will He obtain more glory from Brian's pure testimony of His faithfulness and love in spite of the heartache of his predicament? Only God knows. But He *does* know.

We pray in faith, believing for Brian's healing, knowing full well that God can do anything. At the same time, we submit our request to God's sovereignty. We also pray that God will strengthen Brian's inner-soul capacity, trusting that he will cling fiercely to God's promises and not focus on the questions of "fairness."

Either way provides the opportunity to give God all the glory and honor; supernatural physical healing or personal response to His equally supernatural provision of patience and trust. It is a double-win situation. This principle holds true in every circumstance that happens to us, whether good or bad, "fair" or "unfair."

Meanwhile, Brian is content. He has joined Chuck Swindoll in claiming these two truths that come from the book *Improving Your Serve:*

1. Nothing touches me that has not passed through the hands of my heavenly Father. Nothing.
2. Everything I endure is designed to prepare me for serving others more effectively. Everything.[1]

Brian refuses to let anything or anyone rob him of his joy. In fact, his passion for playing practical jokes and tricks on unsuspecting victims almost borders on terrorist activity. "Ouch! There he goes again — over my toes!"

Submitting to God's sovereignty keeps us in the position of humble servants who are available, with tender hearts to serve Him regardless of the uncontrollable, life-changing events that help determine our lot in life. We choose to draw our water from the well that never runs dry. We studiously avoid the satanic snares of trying to evaluate the "fairness" of our particular set of circumstances and comparing our lives with those of others.

Any approach other than that of yielding to His sovereignty leaves us high and dry. Either we drown in a pool of rationalized self-pity or we become little monsters demanding that God serve us at our bidding. Of course, these routes cause us to forfeit the privilege of seeing the fourth Man in the furnace and cause us to relinquish the joy of seeing hungry lions get their mouths shut. We go through life being pulled by our own ego needs, wants and demands.

God knows our *true* need. For some of us, the need is
for one or more inexplicable, earth-shaking situation(s) that
captures our attention and causes us to focus on eternal values
like never before. For others, the need may be different. We
may not pass through such intense encounters with pain. Oh
yes, we hurt at times and it is the same type of pain, but
the outward circumstances may be less dramatic.

God can deliver, but sometimes he won't. Why? Because
He is working all things together for His purpose. And our
response? Trust. Humble, child-like trust.

Is God "fair"? No, not from our limited, earthly perspective.
But is He just and merciful? Absolutely.

Remember, we are just *passing through* this period of
"child-training" here on earth.

While we continue to be responsible with our daily tasks,
let's keep our eyes upon the glory of the hereafter regardless
of the seeming "unfairness" of God in the present. God is not
"fair." He is just! Period.

> Humble yourselves, therefore, under God's mighty hand,
> that He may lift you up in due time. Cast all your anxiety
> on him because he cares for you.
> Be self-controlled and alert. Your enemy the devil prowls
> around like a roaring lion looking for someone to devour.
> Resist him, standing firm in the faith, because you know
> that your brothers throughout the world are undergoing
> the same kind of suffering.
> And the God of all grace, who called you to his eternal
> glory in Christ, after you have suffered a little while,
> will himself restore you and make you strong, firm, and
> steadfast. To him be the power forever and ever. Amen.
>
> (1 Peter 5:6-11, NIV)

DISCUSSION GUIDE

1. What does God's sovereignty mean to you?

2. List three fears you have about the future. After each,
write these words: GOD IS IN CONTROL.

3. If you have the assurance that God has a plan for
your life, you will see all that comes into your life as the
outworking of His grand design. Remember, He is the master

weaver, and we see the tapestry of life as seemingly tangled threads from the reverse side. He sees the beautiful pattern He is working in and through us.

Epilogue

Why?

I have sat beside a tiny crib,
And watched a baby die,
As parents slowly turned toward me,
To ask, "Oh, pastor, why?"

I have held the youthful husband's head,
And felt death's heave and sigh.
A widow looked through tears and said,
"Dear pastor, tell me why?"

I have seen a gold-star mother weep,
And hold a picture nigh
Her lonely breast, and softly ask,
"Why, pastor, why, oh, why?"

I have walked away from babyland,
Where stillborn babies lie.
A mother stretches empty arms,
And asks me, "Pastor, why?"

I have heard the white-tipped tapping cane,
Which leads a blinded eye.
And then a darkened, lonely voice
Cries, "Preacher, show me why."

I have caught a fiancée's burning tears,
And heard her lonely cry.
She held an unused wedding gown,
And shouted, "Pastor, why?"

I have heard the cancer patient say,
"'Tis gain for me to die;"
Then look into his daughter's face,
And mutely whisper, "Why?"

I have seen a father take his life.
A widow stands nearby;
As little children say, "Dear Mom,
The preacher'll tell us why."

I've seen my mother stand beside
Two tiny graves and cry.
And though she'd never let me know,
I knew she wondered, "Why?"

I've heard an orphan faintly say,
Who gazed into the sky,
"Though Mom and Dad have gone away,
My preacher will know why."

I tiptoed to my Father's throne,
So timid and so shy,
To say, "Dear God, some of your own
Are wanting to know why."

I heard Him say so tenderly,
"Their eyes I'll gladly dry,
Though they must look through faith today
Tomorrow they'll know why.

"If now they find the reasons that
Their hopes have gone awry,
In Heaven, they will miss the joy
Of hearing Me tell why."

And so I've found it pleases Him
When I can testify,
"I'll trust my God to do what's best,
And wait to find out why."[1]

                                        Dr. Jack Hyles

Afterword

After reading this book, if you have not made your peace with God, there is one thing that is necessary. This one thing is more necessary than your next breath, because you are only one heartbeat away from death. Having this one thing is more important than having contentment, self-control, answers to all your "why" questions, or relief from all the pain and suffering you may be experiencing at this present time. If you do not have this one thing, even what you seem to have will be taken away for all eternity. I am talking about the gift of God. Consider His gift. He gave himself in the person of His Son.

God's compassion compelled Him to build a bridge of reconciliation to all people without regard to cost. He did not spare His own Son, Jesus Christ, who humbly took the form of a man about 2,000 years ago and satisfied every demand of perfection God required. Then, in order to satisfy the justice of God, the sins of all of us were laid upon Christ so we would not have to suffer the eternal consequences of our sins.

Jesus voluntarily suffered horrible anguish for us by being nailed to a wooden cross and dying in our place. He was buried, rose again the third day and ascended into heaven, representing the whole world with His precious blood.

He has forgiven your sins; in fact, there is nothing about your past that shocks Him. He has provided meaning for the emotional agony you have endured in your lifetime. He has exhibited His genuine friendship by dying for you, in your place, with no strings attached.

There is nothing more important than being honest about your need to receive the free gift of eternal life by inviting Jesus to come and live inside your heart. The issue is not what you can do to earn God's favor, but what He has already done for you in expressing His unconditional love to you.

Come to Him right now, just as you are, by simple faith and pray:

> Dear God, thank you for sending your Son, Jesus, to die on the cross in my place for my sins. I now accept the fact that the shed blood of Jesus has cleansed me from all unrighteousness. I receive Jesus Christ into my heart as the Lord of my life. I want to live for Him for the rest of my life. Thank you for accepting me just as I am. In Jesus' name. Amen.

If you prayed this prayer, please feel free to contact me for some helpful information about your new life in Christ. Enclose a self-addressed, stamped envelope and send it to: P.O. Box 2757, Columbia, MD 21045.

APPENDIX A

Finding Meaning in Pain

The following definitions are not meant to cover the whole gamut of theological knowledge. They are not ponderous explanations, merely vignettes of truth to spice up our understanding during trying times.

● *Affliction:* to experience continued distress and anguish due to the pressure of circumstances, or the antagonism of people; generally that which comes from without and burdens the human soul; the opportunity provided by God to step outside of the debilitating effects of personal wounds and because of the creation of an enlarged capacity of understanding to help others cope.

> *Isaiah 48:10:* "Behold, I have refined thee . . . I have chosen thee in the furnace of affliction."

● *Bitterness:* the attitude of mind characterized by spite, maliciousness, hostility, jealousy, revenge, or hatred and caused by deep emotional roots of insecurity or inadequacy; resentment, whether disguised or openly exhibited, may develop as the result of loss, deprivation, rejection, or damaged self-esteem; the fruit of long-term preoccupation with the seeming unfairness of certain experiences of life or with death.

> *Hebrews 12:15:* "Looking diligently . . . lest any root of bitterness springing up trouble you, and thereby many be defiled."

● *Carefree:* the courageous attitude of mind which allows one to confront the painful responsibilities of life head-on without anxiety or a falsely based sense of security; the pleasant liberation from the disquieted state of mental distractions, uncertainty or fear regardless of the circumstances; the relaxation of the mental attitudes that results from "slamming" all anxious concerns upon Christ, because of the knowledge of His personal concern and His ability to handle all human problems.

> *1 Peter 5:7:* "Casting all your care upon him; for he careth for you."

● *Comfort:* the type of encouragement and support that brings strengthening aid rather than sympathy and pity; the ability to listen and impart cheer; genuine care for people.

> *Psalm 23:4:* ". . . thy rod and thy staff they comfort me."

• *Commitment:* the moment-by-moment dedication of yourself to the Lordship of Christ, to the completion of the tasks assigned, and to true friendship to the face and behind the back of others in your sphere of influence; setting the sights high when self-pity strikes; aspiring to excel when the wind has been knocked out of your sails; doing the details with dignity, with God as your audience.

1 *Corinthians 15:58:* ". . . be ye steadfast, unmoveable, always abounding in the work of the Lord, for asmuch as ye know that your labour is not in vain in the Lord."

• *Covenant:* the gracious agreement designed by God for the benefit and blessing of people; the binding pledge God has made to us, stating that He will never leave us nor forsake us; the solemn promise that He is for us, not against us; the result being that we can trust Him, even if all hell breaks loose.

Isaiah 54:9: "For this is as the waters of Noah unto me; for as I have sworn that the waters of Noah should no more go over the earth; so have I sworn that I would not be wroth with thee, nor rebuke thee."

• *Crisis:* any experience with a person, place or thing that challenges your structured mentality and forces you to change; the greater the change, the more opportunity for intense emotional pain; without it we remain spiritually immature; with it comes the opportunity to expand our horizons with the experience of rare qualities like compassion, self-control, tolerance, sensitivity, patience, concentration, unselfishness and true friendship; any challenge to grow, brilliantly disguised as an insurmountable problem.

Psalm 55:19: "Because they have no changes, therefore they fear not God."

• *Delight:* applied to the human will, it implies entire and full inclination toward pleasing and honoring the Lord, regardless of the circumstances.

Psalm 40:8: "I delight to do thy will, O my God."

• *Discipline:* the gracious but firm training and instruction that is given to God's children; sometimes it is difficult to bear, but if the recipient is entreatable, it softens the heart and directs the way; the pain God uses to guide us back within the boundary lines of our inheritance; "Lord, I don't want the rod again, not the major chastisement. Just a little tap will do and I will respond quickly! You are the Boss. I am Your willing servant."

> *Hebrews 12:11:* "Now no chastening for the present seemeth to be joyous, but grievous: nevertheless afterward it yieldeth the peaceable fruit of righteousness unto them which are exercised thereby."

● *Encouragement:* the inspiration of courage, confidence, and purpose in the Lord; the realization that you are on the road to ultimate triumph; strengthens self-discipline and prompts an attitude of stick-to-itiveness in the darkest hour.

> *1 Samuel 30:6:* "And David was greatly distressed . . . but David encouraged himself in the Lord his God."

● *Fairness:* the system of perception that fosters self-pity, disillusionment and griping; causes us to compare our life's experience with others so that we either feel superior or inferior; ultimately results in cursing God for His lack of concern and motivates us to question His integrity.

> *Judges 17:6:* "Every man did that which was right [fair] in his own eyes."

● *Faith:* the firm persuasion and conviction, based on hearing, that produces a full acknowledgment of God's truth; a personal surrender to Jesus Christ with personal conduct inspired by such surrender; the telescope that brings the "Heavenly Object" into clear focus; the provision from God to finish the course with sustained vigor and enthusiasm.

> *Hebrews 11:1:* "Now faith is the substance of things hoped for, the evidence of things not seen."

● *Glory:* the brilliant brightness and majestic honor of Jesus Christ that is given to believers immediately upon entrance into heaven; when weighed in the eternal balances, all earthly suffering and pain will be as nothing in sharp contrast to the dazzling light and blinding illumination that will be bursting forth from our heavenly bodies forever and ever; the condition of supreme exaltation and splendor shared with Jesus as a reward for quiet, constant faithfulness to Him while living in the limitations of our earthly bodies.

> *Romans 8:18:* "For I reckon that the sufferings of this

present time are not worthy to be compared with the glory which shall be revealed in us."

● *Grace:* God's Riches At Christ's Expense; the specific, tailor-made provision for every facet of our lives — free, without obligation; permits us to serve Him willingly without trying to earn brownie points; opposite of man's system of legalism and merit; when we experience tragedy, sin, or victory, there is a side of His unmerited grace to keep our hearts on fire with devotion for the One who knows everything about us and still loves us.

2 Peter 3:18: "But grow in grace, and in the knowledge of our Lord and Savior Jesus Christ. To him be glory both now and for ever. Amen."

● *Grief:* emotional response of panic, despair, remorse or bereavement to the life-shattering shock of a loss; tears apart one's former patterns of life, either forces one to be absorbed in the passion of hope and growth or causes one to shift toward cynicism or despair; lively hope in Christ is the anchor that halts the natural drift toward groans of sorrow and despair.

Isaiah 53:3: "He is despised and rejected of men; a man of sorrows, and acquainted with grief."

● *Humility:* the liberation from pride or arrogance; the courage to risk, the confidence in Christ during failure, the boldness to receive forgiveness, and the freedom to risk again without condemnation; God's provision which keeps us from pinheadedness in defeat, swell-headedness in victory, and which causes us to maintain our sense of humor through it all.

Galatians 6:14: "But God forbid that I should glory, save in the cross of our Lord Jesus Christ, by whom the world is crucified unto me, and I unto the world."

● *Joy:* gladness, jubilation and exultation over the fact that God has everything under control, regardless of how current circumstances may appear; this mental attitude depends entirely upon trusting God's promises and is not dependent on health, job conditions, home environment or financial status; experiences of sorrow or persecution prepare for and enlarge the capacity for this settled state of mind; since happiness depends upon circumstances, happiness and depression cannot co-exist, but joy and suffering can and do.

2 Corinthians 7:4: "I am filled with comfort, I am exceeding joyful in all our tribulation."

● *Justice:* the application of God's holy character to the affairs of human beings; the principle which exhibits that the perfect ability of God's power or omnipotence can do anything, but also reveals that His sovereignty sometimes leaves a Daniel in the lion's den or allows a Job to suffer inexplicable tragedy — all for His glory as a part of the infinite wisdom of His plan; humans who dare to trust His character will experience untold blessing within, regardless of the fury of the storms without; the principle that caused God, the Father, to be pleased when His only Son, Jesus, was crucified for the sins of the whole world, thereby satisfying His justice.

Psalm 89:14: "Justice and judgment are the habitation of thy throne."

● *Meditation:* continued contemplation and reflection on specific passages from the Holy Scriptures, allowing the Word to get a firm grasp on you; strengthens prayer life; sharpens witnessing; enhances confidence; solidifies faith in God; causes your counsel to be in demand.

Joshua 1:8: "This book of the law shall not depart out of thy mouth; but thou shalt meditate therein day and night, that thou mayest observe to do according to all that is written therein: for then thou shalt make thy way prosperous, and then thou shalt have good success."

● *Mercy:* the adequate expression of God's resource of compassion, kindness and forgiveness toward sinful mankind that functions in perfect harmony with His infallible justice.

Lamentations 3:22-23: "It is of the Lord's mercies that we are not consumed, because his compassions fail not. They are new every morning: great is thy faithfulness."

● *Pain:* the state of emotional distress ranging from mild annoyance to unbearably acute agony; the goad that makes us willing to leave this world; without heartache we would be perfectly content to remain on earth forever; the opportunity to receive God's specific provision of victory over the predictable intrusions of resentment, frustration and disappointment; the agent God uses to soften the heart, dislodging the temporal values and infusing the eternal.

Hosea 6:1: "He hath torn, and he will heal us; he hath

smitten, and he will bind us up."

● *Patience:* calm endurance and quiet persistence under the most severe of pressures without complaining; it keeps you on your feet, walking forward with your face toward the wind; it causes you to see the eternal goal beyond the temporal pain, thereby transforming every potential stumbling stone into a stepping stone; it enables you to face oppression without retaliation, delay without depression and suffering without fainting; learned from Christ who doesn't give up on us in our failure, weakness and selfishness.

> *James 1:4:* "But let patience have her perfect work, that ye may be perfect [mature] and entire [complete], wanting nothing."

● *Peace:* the mental and spiritual condition that is free from clamorous, confused thoughts or emotions; the tranquil state of the soul that inhales God's perspective from the Scriptures and exhales quietness and confidence in the midst of potentially upsetting events; the conviction that when, not if, the enemy comes in like a flood — the Lord sits on the flood.

> *Philippians 4:11:* "For I have learned, in whatsoever state I am, therewith to be content."

● *Prayer:* the continual heart cry of a desperate person who despises spiritual complacency and stagnation; the disciplined, unceasing consciousness of Almighty God's willingness to help in good times as well as bad; the call for reckless abandonment of our wills to the joyful discovery of His will; the acid test of true devotion to the Lordship of Christ.

> *Luke 18:1:* "Men ought always to pray, and not to faint."

● *Pride:* the blind, inordinate preoccupation with the needs, wants and desires of self, attended with rude, insolent attitudes toward others; anxiety to gain approval from others, with unreasonable rage and distress exhibited when slighted; the parent of criticism, discontent, presumption, lust, ingratitude and bigotry; the excessive guilt or condemnation that arises when one assumes his sins are greater than God's grace, while succumbing to pressure or adversity — which shows that one assumes his sufferings are greater than God's provision — both being disguised forms of haughtiness; smashed at the foot of Calvary.

1 *Peter 5:5:* "God resisteth the proud, and giveth grace
to the humble."

● *Rationalization:* highly systemized and intricate thought patterns, one leading logically to the next, that assist a person in avoiding
clear-cut, unwavering obedience to the specific mandate of the Bible;
"I've always been like that. I guess I'll never change. Oh, that's just
me." Such excuses encourage one to diminish or completely ignore
the Holy Spirit's work of conviction and shave the edge off of
disobedience.

James 4:17: "Therefore to him that knoweth to do good
and doeth it not, to him it is sin."

● *Resist:* to appropriate the power provided because of an
empty cross and an empty tomb — to withstand the force of the
propaganda from this present evil world; to stand against the insistent
demands from our old selfish natures; to be able to repel and ward
off the fiery darts from the wicked one, Satan; to have the guts to
counteract self-pity, anger and resentment.

James 4:7: "Submit yourselves therefore to God. Resist
the devil, and he will flee from you."

● *Sublimation:* the excessive pursuit of socially acceptable behavior like sports, career, hobbies, or religious activity accompanied
by the lack of confrontation with deep root problems in the soul (a
husband and wife extra-busy with separate interests so they don't
have to face the mounting conflicts in their marital relationship); the
avoidance of an honest, transparent relationship with the Holy Spirit.

Hebrews 4:12: "For the word of God is quick, and
powerful, and sharper than any two-edged sword, piercing
even to the dividing asunder of the soul and spirit, and
of the joints and marrow, and is a discerner of the
thoughts and intents of the heart."

● *Tears:* the concentrated portrait of the deepest longings of
the human soul; the language spoken by the joy of fulfilled desires,
the heartache of thwarted love, remorse over personal sin, the gnawing
physical pain from accident or disease, or loss of loved one; the
school of weeping provides the opportunity to feel our utter, sweet
dependence upon God and to learn the art of comforting the
brokenhearted; the leaky head never swells up.

Revelation 21:4: "And God shall wipe away all tears from their eyes; and there shall be no more death, neither sorrow, nor crying, neither shall there be any more pain: for the former things are passed away."

● *Thankfulness:* the secret of mental and spiritual health; the attitude of gratitude; continual consciousness of the blessings and benefits received from the hand of God; when everything is going crazy, it's the disciplined awareness that God is good, He never changes, and that there is always something and Someone to appreciate.

Ephesians 5:20: "Giving thanks always for all things unto God and the Father in the name of our Lord Jesus Christ."

● *Trial:* the fiery tests, designed for passing grades, not failure, that determine the inclinations of our hearts; positive inclinations toward God reveal acceptable, approved, trustworthy servants; events acting as compliments from God, indicating His awareness that we are truly mature enough to handle more intense heat; the process of proving and testing.

Job 23:10: "When he hath tried me, I shall come forth as gold."

● *Trust:* intelligent — not blind — confidence in the character and integrity of Jesus Christ; reliance on His promises even when doubts about His dependability assail us; the ability to love again after the heart has been broken.

Psalm 62:8: "Trust in him at all times; ye people, pour out your heart before him: God is a refuge for us. Selah."

APPENDIX B

The Conflict Between "Fairness" Versus Justice and Mercy

The following material, is an excerpt from The Unexpected Enemy of Justice and Mercy published by The Institute in Basic Youth Conflicts. The material clearly defines the conflict between "fairness" versus justice and mercy.[1]

JUSTICE AND MERCY	vs. "FAIRNESS"
1. Justice is based on the the universal, unchangeable principles of God's Word. EXAMPLE: *God alone is the giver of life. No individual has the right to destroy it at his or her own whim. (See Exodus 10:13.)*	1. "Fairness" is based on variable customs of a society and the changing will of the majority. EXAMPLE: *"Fairness" laws now give mothers the right to decide whether or not they want their unborn children to live.*
2. Justice establishes guilt when God's standards are violated. EXAMPLE: *God states that every person must be responsible for his or her own thoughts, words, and actions. (See Matthew 5: 21-22.)*	2. "Fairness" tries to remove guilt by lowering God's standards. EXAMPLE: *A judge in Wisconsin excused a high school boy for raping a girl on the basis that the boy had been subjected to sensual stimuli in our society and was only doing what was natural.*
3. Justice causes us to confess our failures and plead for mercy. EXAMPLE: *A convicted murderer may be shown mercy and be pardoned. (See 1 John 1:9-10.)*	3. "Fairness" causes us to justify our failures so that we do not think that we need mercy. EXAMPLE: *"Fairness" laws do not convict a murderer who successfully argues "temporary insanity."*
4. Justice and mercy are based on personal responsibility to a holy God, and they	4. "Fairness" is based on personal rights, and it will produce rebellion within a

will produce revival in a nation.

EXAMPLE: *When God's law was read to the kingdom of Judah during Josiah's reign, the people wept, confessed their sin, and turned back God. (See 2 Kings 22-23.)*

5. Justice is based on protecting eternal values.
EXAMPLE: *Truthfulness and loyalty to sacred vows are more important than personal pleasure. (See Ecclesiastes 5:4.)*

6. Justice emphasizes personal responsibility.
EXAMPLE: *Every person is responsible for his or her every thought. If a man has lustful thoughts toward a woman, he is already guilty of adultery with her in his heart. (See Matthew 5:27-32.)*

7. Justice is the expression of God's wisdom for our nation, and its application will lead to prosperity.
EXAMPLE: *If God's principles of finance were followed, a nation's welfare needs would be met by individuals, families, employers, and charitable institutions, not by the government. (See*

nation.

EXAMPLE: *"Fairness" legislation now calls sodomy a "victimless crime." The fact is that it unleashes passions which damage others and bring God's judgment on the entire community.*

5. "Fairness" is based on protecting temporal values.
EXAMPLE: *"Fairness" laws on divorce and remarriage are based on the assumption that personal happiness is more important than being truthful and loyal to marriage vows.*

6. "Fairness" emphasizes personal rights.
EXAMPLE: *"Fairness" laws on pornography conclude that every person has a personal right to read whatever he or she wants to read. "Fairness" laws claim that morality cannot be legislated. The fact is that every law is legislating morality. The only question is, whose morality — God's or man's?*

7. "Fairness" is the expression of human reasoning for a nation, and its application will lead to financial ruin.
EXAMPLE: *"Fairness" laws are taking more and more rights from parents, churches, and businesses. As a result, the government is assuming an overwhelming responsibility for*

Deuteronomy 28:1-14.)

the social welfare of its
citizens. The possible col-
lapse of the entire system
is now a real concern to
those who are depending on
it.

8. Justice is impartial. It is
objective and non-emotional.
ILLUSTRATION: *The impar-
tiality of justice is
expressed by the blindfold
on the statue of Justice.
God warns that we should not
show favoritism to either the
rich or the poor. (See
Exodus 23:2-3.)*

8. "Fairness" is partial. It
is subjective and based on
arbitrary emotional con-
sideration.
*EXAMPLE: In trying to
enforce traffic laws
"fairly," a California
policeman testified, 'I
have found that when I
attempt to be 'fair,' I
inevitably cite those who
should have been warned,
and warn those who should
have been cited."*

9. Justice results in the swift
prosecution of criminals.
*REASON: "Because sentence
against an evil work is not
executed speedily, therefore
the heart of the sons of men
is fully set in them to do
evil" (Ecclesiastes 8:11).*

9. "Fairness" results in
the slow prosecution of
criminals.
*EXAMPLE: "Fairness" laws
allow convicted criminals
to evade the consequences
of their actions by con-
centrating too heavily on
the procedural maneuvers of
the accused, even if the
accused is clearly guilty.
This results in frivolous
technicalities and con-
tinuous appeals at the
taxpayers' expense.*

10. Justice limits the punishment of a criminal.
*EXAMPLE: "An eye for an
eye, and a tooth for a
tooth" (Matthew 5:38), puts
limitations on punishment.
By the time of Christ, the
true meaning of this law
had become distorted.*

10. "Fairness"results in the
inconsistent punishment of
a criminal.
*EXAMPLE: "Fairness" laws
will often overreact to
parents who spank their
children, while neglecting
drug pushers and porno-
graphy pushers who violate
the morals of children.*

11. Justice establishes God's view of what is essential for a nation to be successful. EXAMPLE: *God places great value on the life and worth of an individual. He requires punishment for anyone who murders another person: "Whoso sheddeth man's blood, by man shall his blood be shed: for in the image of God made he man" (Genesis 9:6).*

12. Justice allows an employer to be generous to those who are in special need. EXAMPLE: *After paying agreed-upon wages, an employer may wish to give an extra amount to someone in need. (See Proverbs 14:21.)*

13. Justice holds the individual guilty for his offense. EXAMPLE: *Ananias and Sapphira lied to the Holy Spirit and kept back part of the price of the land they had sold. Because of this, God took their lives (Acts 5:1-11). "The soul that sinneth, it shall die . . ." (Ezekiel 18:20).*

11. "Fairness" establishes man's view of what is essential for a nation to be successful. EXAMPLE: *"Fairness" laws make it legal to kill millions of unborn children, our national heritage; but they bring swift, harsh fines and imprisonment for killing an endangered species such as our national bird, the eagle.*

12. "Fairness" legislates against an employer's being generous with those who are in need. EXAMPLE: *"Fairness" laws require employers to give each person in a given job classification the same pay, regardless of individual need.*

13. Humanistic laws based on "fairness" hold society guilty for an individual's offense. EXAMPLE: *The "fairness" penal code of our day is based upon the philosophy that the criminal needs to be rehabilitated, at the taxpayers' expense, rather than making restitution for his crime. A legislator in Colorado has determined that in his state it would cost the taxpayers less to send every prisoner to Harvard than to incarcerate them!*[1]

APPENDIX C

Suffering: A Biblical Survey

Suffering: A Biblical Survey was the original resource material used in the promotion of the movie *Joni.* It is the most complete, concise study I have ever seen on the subject of suffering. I thank World Wide Pictures for permission to reprint this valuable work.[1]

A. BIBLICAL PRINCIPLES RELATED TO SUFFERING

After each principle there are letters to indicate to whom it applies: G-general/B-believers/U-unbelievers.

1. Suffering cannot always be said to be caused by sin or to indicate lack of spiritually (1 Corinthians 4:9-14; John 9:1-3; 2 Corinthians 11:22-31). G
2. The source of suffering is linked with sin, evil, and the curse of God (Genesis 3:14-19; 1 Corinthians 15:51-55; Romans 8:20-23). G
3. Removal of suffering is linked with redemption (Genesis 3:21 — c.f. context of curse prior to this verse) and the ultimate triumph of righteousness (2 Peter 3:5-7,10; Revelation 21:1,4 and 22:2,3). G
4. Suffering and evil occur in the broader context of God's providence (Genesis 50:20; Job 1:12; 2:6). It is not fate or bad luck. G
5. Suffering can be negative or positive, depending on how you respond (Genesis 50:20; book of Job). Satan wants to turn us aside (1 Peter 5:8,9); God wants sufferings to strengthen us (Job). G
6. Suffering is to be anticipated in the light of God's character (1 Peter 4:19; Job 23:10-13,14; 1 Corinthians 10:13; Isaiah 55:9, Ecclesiastes 11:5) so that we should not fall prey to despair (2 Corinthians 4:8, Romans 8:28-32, 37-39). G
7. Suffering indicates the vulnerability of our present state and the need for redemption (2 Corinthians 5:1-5; Philippians 3:21). This points out that man's greatest need is not just salvation of the body, but

of the soul which continues past the grave (1 Peter 1:6,9,24). G

8. Suffering tests where our real point of hope is (1 Peter 1:6,13) and reveals the intent of our hearts (Job's wife, Job 2:9; Psalm 11:5, 17:1-5) because it makes us reflect on the real meaning of life (see the Psalms). G

9. Suffering is used to increase our awareness of the sustaining power of God and to whom we owe our sustenance (Psalm 68:19; 2 Corinthians 12:9,10), and draws us closer to Him (Job 23:5,7,10) because He cares for us (1 Peter 5:7). G

10. God uses suffering to gain the praises of men both good and evil (1 Peter 1:6,7; John 9:1-3, 11:4; Revelation 11:13). G

11. God uses suffering to refine, perfect, strengthen and keep us from falling (Psalm 66:8,9; Hebrews 2:10, 12:10). B

12. Suffering allows the life of Christ to be manifested in our mortal flesh (2 Corinthians 4:7-11) bankrupting us, making us dependent on God (2 Corinthians 12:9; Psalm 14:6). B

13. Suffering teaches us humility (2 Corinthians 12:7), imparting the mind of Christ (Philippians 2:1-11), for God is more concerned with character than comfort (Romans 5:3,4; Hebrews 12:10,11). Thus, the greatest good of the Christian life is not absence of pain but Christ-likeness (2 Corinthians 4:8-10; Romans 8:28,29). B

14. Suffering can be a chastisement from God for sin and rebellion (Psalm 107:17; Isaiah 24:5,6; Acts 5:1-11; 1 Corinthians 11:29,30). G

15. Suffering is the only means in which moral evil enters into the consciousness of God (God — Isaiah 63:9; Christ — Luke 9:22, 17:25, 24:26,46; Matthew 16:21; Hebrews 2:10). G

16. Voluntary suffering is one way to demonstrate the love of God (2 Corinthians 8:1,2,9). B

17. Obedience and self-control is learned from suffering (Hebrews 5:8) along with patience (Romans 5:1-5) and refinement (James 1:2-8; Proverbs 17:3), conforming

us to His death (Philippians 3:10, 2:1-11). B

18. Suffering may be due to a failure of ourselves, or failure to employ our God-given resources in accord with wisdom (Proverbs 19:16, 13:20, 11:24, 22:3, 27:12; Job 21). G

19. Temporary suffering may be due to those over us who are negligent (Numbers 14:31-33), but on an ultimate basis we stand as individuals (Ezekiel 18:10 and broad context). G

20. Suffering or pain is an indicator or deterrent to continual bodily harm (Psalm 139). G

21. Suffering is part of the righteousness struggle against sin (Hebrews 12:4-13) and evil men (Psalm 27:12 and 37:14, 15; 1 Peter 2:18, 2 Timothy 3:1-13; Hebrews 11:36-40). See — suffering for righteousness sake, 1 Peter 3:14; for His sake, Philippians 1:29; for the kingdom of God, 2 Thessalonians 1:5; for the Gospel, 2 Timothy 2:9; for unjustness, 1 Peter 2:19; as Christians, 1 Peter 4:16; for the name, Acts 5:41. This indicates how the righteous become sharers in Christ's suffering (2 Corinthians 1:5; 1 Peter 4:13) as sons (1 Peter 5:8; Hebrews 11:36-38). B

22. Satan uses suffering to cast aspersion on the character of God and His saints (Job 1,2). G

23. Suffering serves as a preliminary warning of the judgment to come to unbelievers (Luke 16; Revelation 20:10-15; 2 Kings 15:5). U

24. Satan uses suffering as an obstacle to evangelizing (Ephesians 6:16-20; 2 Timothy 4:1-8, 15-17; 2 Corinthians 4:7-18). B

25. Endurance of suffering is given as a cause for reward (2 Corinthians 4:17; 2 Timothy 2:12). B

26. Suffering demonstrates the total commitment to Christ that we need in all that we do or say (2 Corinthians 4) and demonstrates the need for the grace of God to sustain us. B

27. Suffering forces community and the administration of our gifts for the common good (1 Peter 4:12; 1 Corinthians 12; Philippians 4:12-15). B

28. Suffering indicates that real faith can survive both calamity and prosperity (Job 42:7-17). B

29. Suffering teaches us that sustenance for our lives is not found totally in our physical life but in the inworking of God upon the heart. B

30. Suffering binds Christians together into a common or joint purpose (Revelation 1:9). B

31. Suffering produces discernment and knowledge and teaches us His statutes (Psalm 119:66,67,71). B

32. Through suffering God is able to obtain a broken and contrite spirit which He desires (Psalm 51:16,17; Psalm 32). G

33. Suffering causes us to gird our minds by making us fix our hope on the grace to be revealed at the revelation of Jesus Christ (1 Peter 1:6,13 and 2:5). G

34. Suffering can be used as a nullifier to the counsel of the nations and the frustration of their plans (Revelation 17, 18; Psalm 33:10). U

35. God uses suffering to humble us that He might exalt us at the proper time (1 Peter 5:6,7 and broad context). B

36. Suffering teaches us to number our days that we might present to God a heart of wisdom (Psalm 90:7-12). B

37. Because ultimate judgment is not yet final, current suffering must be viewed as a necessary complement to this life (1 Peter 5:10; Philippians 3:20,21). G

38. Suffering, as a complement to evil, will be the wages of the ungodly for their rebellion (2 Peter 2:13 and 3:7). Therefore, suffering serves as a warning to the ungodly. U

39. Suffering is valuable to godliness when coupled with contentment (1 Timothy 6:6). B

40. Suffering is sometimes necessary to win the lost (2 Timothy 2:8-10 and 4:5,6; 2 Corinthians 1:1-11). B

41. Sufferings of the righteous strengthen and allow one to comfort those who are weak or suffering (Philippians 1:12-14,20 and 2:17; 2 Corinthians 1:3-11 and 7:6,7; Hebrews 2:18). B

42. Suffering is only temporary and in light of its momentary affliction is nothing as compared to the surpassing value of knowing Christ (Philippians 3:8). B

43. Since righteousness does not exempt us from suffer-

ing, this should teach us that there is a warfare going on, on a much higher plane, which, until complete, will allow sufering to continue. G

44. God desires truth in our innermost being and one way He does it is through suffering (Psalm 51:6 and 119:17). B

45. The equity for suffering will be found in the next life (Psalm 58:10,11; Luke 16:19-31, especially verse 25; 1 Peter 2:12). B

46. Suffering is always coupled with a greater source of grace (2 Timothy 1:7,8 and 4:16-18; 1 Peter 4:14; 2 Peter 1:3; 1 Corinthians 10:13). B

47. Suffering can lead to the repentance of sin (Psalm 32; 2 Corinthians 7:5-11). G

48. Suffering teaches us as men that we are frail and weak, dependent for hope on someone greater (Psalm 14:6 and 11:1). G

49. Suffering of the righteous (vengeance) will be a main cause for the judgment of the wicked (Psalm 12:5; Revelation 6:9-11). U

50. Suffering teaches us to give thanks in times of sorrow (2 Corinthians 1:11). B

51. Suffering increases faith (Abraham — Genesis 22; Psalm 46:10; Jeremiah 29:11). B

52. Suffering allows God to manifest His care (Psalm 56:8). B

53. Suffering stretches our hope (Job 13:14-15). B

54. When suffering seems to have no meaning in the physical realm it does have meaning in the spiritual realm (Job 1-3. Remember, Job knew not the cause or reason for his sufferings). G

55. Suffering is used to break the will of the rebellious (Revelation 11:13). Pain plants the flag of reality in the fortress of a rebel heart. C.S. Lewis, "God whispers in our pleasure but shouts in our pain."

56. When there is no answer for the suffering, it does not mean God has forgotten, only that resolution is destined for the life to come (Psalm 9:12,18). G

57. Suffering indicates that true hope changes sorrow but does not obliterate it. G

58. Suffering is not cause for being ashamed (2 Timothy

1:12). B

B. THE PRINCIPLES LOGICALLY APPLIED

As one approaches the subject of suffering within the Scriptures, he finds that the complete "why" of suffering is never found. He must rather rest in the character of God (Deuteronomy 29:29, Isaiah 55:8,9) and that all suffering takes place within the appointed boundaries of God. This does not mean that we are not to pursue the subject, only that we are to bow to the truth which God has given us, with the amount of explanation He has revealed.

As we enter the realm of suffering, we are immediately caught by a foundation principle that human suffering cannot be understood in a purely human or naturalistic context, but must encompass the heavenly counterpart, the spiritual realm. From the physical plane, man finds God trapped in inconsistency; how can a holy God allow evil and any complement of it? Here we must bow to mystery, but not to mystery without direction. For in the question of evil, which poses the greatest threat to God and His character, especially His holiness, we find that He has given us some guidelines to allow us to rest in His revealed character.

1. God's ultimate glory is found with His triumph over all evil and sin and any of its counterparts, such as suffering and wickedness (Revelation 21:1-5).

2. In His triumph, He reveals that suffering is intricately linked with Satan, evil, and the fall (death), and the curse of God upon the earth (Revelation 20:10-15, 21:1-5, 22:1-5; Genesis 3:14-19,21; 2 Peter 3:5-7,10; 1 Corinthians 15:51-55; Romans 8:20-23).

3. He allows evil and suffering only to occur within the broad context of His providence, for God never relinquishes control of His omnipotent rule, which gives hope to those who suffer.

4. That with the entrance of sin and suffering, not all further suffering is due to immediate sin or wrongdoing or serves as an act of punishment, for in the book of Job, the dialogue in heaven has established Job's innocence before God (Job 1:7,8).

5. This means that suffering is a natural counterpart to life within a fallen world. In the end, God will create a new heaven and earth where there are no tears,

death, mourning, crying, or pain; for the first heaven
and earth have passed away with the removal of all
the ungodly, including Satan and his demon host, and
upon the new heaven and earth we will find the godly.
    6. This enlightens us as to five facts:
        a. That God's ultimate justice transcends the earth-
        ly and temporal.
        b. That God is using that which opposes His
        character to glorify Himself (Proverbs 16:4).
        c. That time, which allows for the existence of
        sin and evil, poses no threat to God's character
        as long as victory and equity are assured.
        d. That the ultimate answer to suffering rests in
        the justice, wisdom, and knowledge of a transcen-
        dent God.
        e. That suffering remains because mortality has
        not put on immortality (1 Corinthians 15:51-55).

This means that suffering stands as a neutral test because
two opposing personalities are using it for their own ends,
one for good and one for evil.

Satan uses it to glorify himself by:
    1. Impugning God's character
    2. Opposing the saints
    3. Hindering the work of redemption
    4. Verifying his own power
    5. Causing disunity — the contradiction to a
       harmonious God
    6. Furthering his own kingdom
    7. Nullifying sanctification
God uses it to glorify Himself by:
    1. Using it as a warning device in the physical
       makeup of a man
    2. Bringing joy out of despair
    3. Building character in men
    4. Breaking the will of the ungodly
    5. Sanctifying the inner man
    6. Judging sin with its own product
    7. Eliminating it
    8. Warning man of His ultimate judgment

9. Testing the character of faith in His saints
10. Foiling the counsel of the ungodly
11. Bringing the praise of the wicked in His day of visitation
12. Winning the lost
13. Imparting knowledge of Himself
14. Teaching man dependence on Him
15. Bringing reward
16. Giving us the knowledge of Christ
17. Teaching us to give thanks in all things
18. Disciplining His saints
19. Allowing us to experience more of God's comfort
20. Perceiving the outcome of wrong moral and natural choices

Man may face it by:
1. Wanting to remake the world
2. Anticipating it
3. Crying in self-pity
4. Rebelling against it
5. Resigning oneself to it
6. Looking for God in it
7. Waiting on God even if He's not perceived[1]

APPENDIX D

Bible Bullets

Any one of these "Bible Bullets" will score a direct hit when the enemy attacks with thoughts about God's lack of "fairness." Take time to meditate on these precious Scriptures.

- *Psalm 31:7-8:* I will be glad and rejoice in your love, for you saw affliction and knew the anguish of my soul. You have not handed me over to the enemy but have set my feet in a spacious place (NIV).

- *Psalm 50:15:* Call to me when trouble comes; I will save you, and you will praise me (GNB).

- *Psalm 46:1-5:* God is our shelter and strength, always ready to help in times of trouble. So we will not be afraid, even if the earth is shaken and mountains fall into the ocean depths; even if the seas roar and rage, and the hills shaken by the violence. There is a river that brings joy to the city of God, to the sacred house of the Most High. God is in that city, and it will never be destroyed; at early dawn he will come to its aid (GNB).

- *Habakkuk 3:17-19:* Even though the fig trees have no fruit and no grapes grow on the vines, even though the olive crop fails and the fields produce no grain, even though the sheep all die and the cattle stalls are empty, I will still be joyful and glad, because the LORD God is my Savior. The Sovereign LORD gives me strength. He makes me sure-footed as a deer and keeps me safe on the mountains (GNB).

- *Nahum 1:7:* The LORD is good; he protects his people in times of trouble; he takes care of those who turn to him (GNB).

- *Psalm 55:22:* Cast your cares on the LORD, and he will sustain you; he will never let the righteous fall (NIV).

- *Psalm 34:4-7:* I prayed to the LORD and he answered me; he freed me from all my fears. The oppressed look to him and are glad; they will never be disappointed. The helpless call to him, and he answers; he saves them from all their troubles. His angel guards those who have reverence for the LORD and rescues them from danger (GNB).

- *Isaiah 58:11:* The LORD will guide you always; he will satisfy your needs in a sun-scorched land and will strengthen your frame. You will be like a well-watered garden, like a spring whose waters never fail (NIV).

- *James 1:2-4:* Consider it pure joy, my brothers, whenever you face trials of many kinds, because you know that the testing of your faith develops perseverance. Perseverance must finish its work so that you may be mature and complete, not lacking anything (NIV).

- *2 Corinthians 4:16-18:* For this reason we never become discouraged. Even though our physical being is gradually decaying, yet our spiritual being is renewed day after day. And this small and temporary trouble we suffer will bring us tremendous and eternal glory, much greater than the trouble . . . What can be seen lasts only for a time, but what cannot be seen lasts forever (GNB).

- *Romans 8:18:* I consider that what we suffer at this present time cannot be compared at all with the glory that is going to be revealed to us (GNB).

- *1 Corinthians 15:58:* Therefore, my dear brothers, stand firm. Let nothing move you. Always give yourselves fully to the work of the Lord, because you know that your labor in the Lord is not in vain (NIV).

- *Romans 5:1-5:* Therefore, since we have been justified through faith, we have peace with God through our Lord Jesus Christ, through whom we have gained access by faith into this grace in which we now stand. And we rejoice in the hope of the glory of God. Not only so, but we also rejoice in our own sufferings, because we know that suffering produces perseverance; perseverance, character; and character, hope. And hope does not disappoint us, because God has poured out his love into our hearts by the Holy Spirit, whom he has given us (NIV).

- *2 Corinthians 4:8:* We are often troubled, but not crushed; sometimes in doubt, but never in despair; there are many enemies, but we are never without a friend; and though badly hurt at times, we are not destroyed (GNB).

- *Revelation 20:10:* Then the Devil, who deceived them, was thrown into the lake of fire and sulfur, where the beast and false prophet had already been thrown; and they will be tormented day and night forever and ever (GNB).

- *Job 36:15:* But God teaches men through suffering and uses distress to open their eyes (GNB).

● *Psalm 4:1:* Hear me when I call, O God of my righteousness: thou hast enlarged me when I was in distress . . .

Notes

Chapter 2
1. Paul Malte, *Why Does God Allow Suffering?* (St. Louis: Lutheran Laymen's League, 1965), p. 5.

Chapter 3
1. Anton Szandor LaVey, *The Satanic Bible* (New York: Avon Books, 1969), pp. 30-35.
2. Mick Jagger and Keith Richards, "Sympathy for the Devil," copyright 1968, ABKCO Music, New York City 10019. Used by permission.

Chapter 4
1. W.E. Vine, *An Expository Dictionary of New Testament* Words (Old Tappan, New Jersey: Fleming H. Revell Company), pp. 55-56.
2. Vine, *An . . . Words,* pp. 55-56.

Chapter 8
1. Victor E. Frankl, *Man's Search for Meaning* (New York: Washington Square Press, Inc., 1963), pp. 137-138.
2. Frankl, *Man's . . . Meaning,* p. 121.
3. Frankl, *Man's . . . Meaning,* pp. 124-125.
4. Sabina Wurmbrand, *The Pastor's Wife* (California: Diane Book Publishing, 1985), p. 148.

Chapter 10
1. David Seamands, *Healing for Damaged Emotions* (Wheaton, Illinois: Victor Books, 1981), pp. 14-15.
2. Jill Sciacca, "How to Comfort the Suffering," *Discipleship Journal* (Issue Seventeen, 1983), pp. 36-38.

Chapter 13
1. W.E. Vine, *An Expository Dictionary of New Testament Words* (Old Tappan, New Jersey: Fleming H. Revell Company), p. 130.

Chapter 17
1. Charles R. Swindoll, *Improving Your Serve* (Waco, Texas: Word Books, 1981), p. 189.

Epilogue
1. Jack Hyles, *Please Pardon My Poetry* (Hammond, Indiana: Hyles-Anderson Publishers, 1976), pp. 22-24.

Appendix B
1. "The Conflict Between 'Fairness' versus Mercy and Justice" is published as "The Conflict Between Mercy and Justice versus 'Fairness'," *The Unexpected Enemy of Justice and Mercy* (Supplementary Alumni Book, Volume 8, The Institute in Basic Youth Conflicts, 1982), pp. 6-8. Reprinted and used by permission.

Appendix C
  1. *Suffering: A Biblical Survey* (World Wide Pictures, 1980). Used by permission.

More help for the tough times.

THE ACCLAIMED
"REASON FOR HOPE" SERIES

WHEN YOUR CHILD IS ON DRUGS OR ALCOHOL. Professional counselor Andre Bustanoby shows how to help your child make responsible choices and how to help your child face up to his/her destructive behavior. 951368/$2.95

HELPING TEENS HANDLE STRESS. Marriage and family expert H. Norman Wright addresses one of today's most pressing issues: the stress today's teen encounters through peer pressure, school, and the search for identity. A must for parents and youth workers. 951764/$2.95

HELPING CHILDREN HANDLE STRESS. H. Norman Wright shows how instilling healthy patterns of stress management in young children will help produce a better-adjusted, confident and responsible teenager. A must for parents and children's workers. 951913/$2.95

WHEN YOU'VE BEEN ABUSED. Professional counselor Andre Bustanoby offers practical help for those who have lived with the nightmare of incest or mental/physical/verbal abuse. 951384/$2.95

WHEN YOU HAVE FAILED. If you're discouraged by a recent failure in your life, Andre Bustanoby will show you how to use the situation as a stepping stone to great accomplishment. 951350/$2.95

WHEN YOU'VE BEEN WRONGED. Professional counselors Frank Minirth and Paul Meier offer effective strategies to help you overcome the hurt and bitterness of being wronged by another person. *Available August 1988.* 952077/$2.95

**AVAILABLE AT YOUR CHRISTIAN BOOKSTORE,
OR CALL HERE'S LIFE PUBLISHERS AT (800)-854-5659.
CALIFORNIA RESIDENTS CALL (714) 886-7981.**